Simply Darwin

Simply Darwin

MICHAEL RUSE

SIMPLY CHARLY
NEW YORK

Contents

Praise for *Simply Darwin*

"Written in a direct, funny and compelling style, *Simply Darwin* is simply Michael Ruse at his best, distilling a complicated history or idea to its essential features so that it is readily comprehended. The reader will be impressed with his synthesizing ability and his talent to develop conceptions that seem irresistible—even if, on due reflection, you want to resist."

–Robert J. Richards, Fishbein Professor of the History of Science, University of Chicago

"In his inimitable style, Michael Ruse—one of the world's foremost experts on the history of evolution—provides an entertaining, stimulating, and provocative account of the life and legacy of Charles Darwin. This is one of the best short summaries of the topic available. Highly recommended especially for students and general readers."

–David Sepkoski, Research Scholar, Max Planck Institute for the History of Science

"An excellent sprint through the highlights of Darwin's life and work. Ruse is a masterful writer who presents a clear account of who Darwin was and why he was important. It's the connection to larger questions of our lives that makes this book a success. Well done, Ruse!"

–Joe Cain, Professor of History and Philosophy of Biology, University College London

"Anyone interested in Darwin, the man and his ideas, will find this an engaging read. No other book provides such a rich account of Darwin and his transforming theory in a colloquial manner, and yet is faithful to the historical details and the philosophical depth of his contribution to science."

—Paul Thompson, Professor in the Institute for the History and Philosophy of Science and Technology, University of Toronto

Other *Great Lives*

Series Editor's Foreword

S imply Charly's "Great Lives" series offers brief but authoritative introductions to the world's most influential people—scientists, artists, writers, economists, and other historical figures whose contributions have had a meaningful and enduring impact on our society.

Each book provides an illuminating look at the works, ideas, personal lives, and the legacies these individuals left behind, also shedding light on the thought processes, specific events and experiences that led these remarkable people to their groundbreaking discoveries or other achievements. Additionally, every volume explores various challenges they had to face and overcome to make history in their respective fields, as well as the little-known character traits, quirks, strengths and frailties, myths and controversies that sometimes surrounded these personalities.

Our authors are prominent scholars and other top experts who have dedicated their careers to exploring each facet of their subjects' work and personal lives.

Unlike many other works that are merely descriptions of the major milestones in a person's life, the "Great Lives" series goes above and beyond the standard format and content. It brings substance, depth, and clarity to the sometimes-complex lives and works of history's most powerful and influential people.

We hope that by exploring this series, readers will not only gain new knowledge and understanding of what drove these geniuses, but also find inspiration for their own lives. Isn't this what a great book is supposed to do?

Charles Carlini, Simply Charly
New York City

Preface

This is a book on Charles Darwin. One is tempted to say, this is "yet another book on Charles Darwin." If you have any doubts, go to *Amazon.com* and type in "Charles Darwin." You get 21,549 results. To put things in perspective, if you type in "Michael Ruse" you get 623 results, and I bet most of those are a function of the fact I share my name with the English word for a trick, a "ruse."

So why yet another book on Charles Darwin? Partly because it is a good tale to tell—a rich young man, of apparently rather modest talents, who travels to faraway lands, upon coming back to England, finds one of the most significant theories in the whole of science. And partly because, even today, there is new material coming out, which changes or modifies our views. The latest finding, for instance, is that Darwin may have been lactose intolerant. This has implications for the way we understand him and his theory. Did he spend his life cowering in a rural village avoiding company, racked with psychosomatic pain from the stress of having discovered a theory that was to get so hostile a reaction from his society? Or were Darwin's ailments a matter of simple physiology and coming to and holding his theory was no great strain at all? And does this tell us something about both Darwin and the society in which he lived, namely that however major the coming of evolution might have been, it was not something that would universally be considered threatening or even unwelcome?

The tale is worth retelling because history is never just one fact after another. One writes it and shapes it, according to our interests. The truth is that today, especially in America, Darwin's ideas are highly controversial, primarily because they are taken to oppose the widespread commitment to a form of evangelical Christianity. I will probably not make many converts, especially among older people, but if some young people read this book and decide that it is a more interesting and challenging world than they have so far been led to think, that in itself is a good reason for the book.

I am grateful to a number of people. First, obviously, to Charles Carlini, editor and publisher of this book, for asking me to contribute to the series about influential historical figures, and also for the help given by him and his co-workers in getting the manuscript ready for publication. Special thanks are due to Helena Bachmann the copy editor. As always, Martin Young, my illustrator, has done a very professional job. I am indebted to my fellow laborers in the so-called "Darwin Industry," and most especially to those with whom I have the greatest disagreements. So much of our work is, in fact, a collaborative effort and without their insights and generosity, my book simply could not have been written. Mark Borrello and David Sepkoski, two of today's best historians of biology, read the manuscript for me, and I thank them for doing so. I owe much to my home institution of Florida State University and especially to the gift of William and Lucyle Werkmeister that funds my professorship. I give particular thanks to Hendrik Geyer, his colleagues, and his staff, at the Stellenbosch Institute for Advanced Study in the wine-growing area of South Africa where I spent a semester, away from the distractions of the real world. I have never had such a wonderful environment, during and after the working hours. Lizzie, my wife, as always makes it all worthwhile.

Michael Ruse
Tallahassee, Florida

1. The Man and His Life

Although Charles Darwin was a great revolutionary—in fact, there are few human beings who have had the same effect on the field of biology and culture, in general—he was not a rebel. He came from a very comfortable, moneyed segment of British society, at a time when Great Britain was the most powerful nation on earth.

Born on February 12, 1809, Charles Robert Darwin was the fourth of five children (and the second of two sons) of Dr. Robert Darwin, a physician in the town of Shrewsbury, in the British Midlands, and his wife, Susannah. His paternal grandfather, Dr. Erasmus Darwin, was a physician too, and also an inventor. His maternal grandfather, Josiah Wedgwood, founded the pottery firm bearing his name; Wedgwood porcelain is still manufactured today, although few people know about the company's link to Darwin.

Because his father was not only successful in his profession but also a talented financier, and because his mother received a large dowry from her father, young Charles never had to work during his lifetime. He fell comfortably into the role expected of him: that of a respectable, upper-middle-class Englishman.

To understand Charles Darwin and his great achievements we should look at the influences around him. There is nothing new in Darwin's work. And yet the work itself was entirely new!

This is a portrait of Charles Darwin, drawn by George Richmond around 1840 when Darwin was thirty, to commemorate his wedding. The excellent quality of the portrait – Richmond was the best in England – reflects the fact that Darwin came from a very wealthy upper-middle-class family.

Before evolution

Charles's father was naturally concerned that his young son would become an idle wastrel. Therefore, when the lad was still in his teens, Robert pushed Charles towards medicine. However, after two years of study in the Scottish capital of Edinburgh, Charles realized that he had no interest in following in his father's footsteps and becoming a doctor. Looking for an alternative, and somewhat in despair, Robert directed Charles towards the church (which is ironic, considering that later on Darwin's theory of evolution would put him at odds with many people's understanding of religious doctrine). In order to become a clergyman in the Church of England, a degree from a British university was required. Therefore, in 1828, Charles enrolled at Christ's College in Cambridge.

He spent three happy years as an undergraduate. His formal courses were not onerous, and he had time to pursue the study of biology, an interest that was growing strongly. However, Darwin's first explorations as a full-time scientist came in the area of geology. In 1831, he had the offer to go as the captain's companion on board the British warship HMS *Beagle*. The ship, under the command of Capt. Robert FitzRoy, was going down to the southern hemisphere to map the coastline of South America. FitzRoy was looking for a gentleman who could pay for his own mess bills (food and drink), who would be outside the line of command, and with whom he could relax in his spare time. Darwin fit the bill exactly.

Overall, the *Beagle* voyage lasted some five years. It went first across to the east coast of South America, starting with Brazil, and then worked its way down to the very bottom to the snowy lands of Tierra del Fuego. It then sailed up the west coast past Chile, eventually swinging out into the Pacific. It made a visit to the group of islands known as the Galapagos Archipelago, now belonging to Ecuador. Afterward, the *Beagle* went southwest to New Zealand and on to Australia. It then visited South Africa, made a quick trip back to South America, and finally returned to England in the autumn of 1836.

HMS Beagle on which Darwin spent five years, from 1831 to 1836, circumnavigating the globe.

During the voyage, Darwin rapidly progressed from the role of captain's friend to that of ship's naturalist. He made massive collections of plants, rocks, and fossils, as well as animal and bird skins. These samples were sent back to England for cataloging and classification. At the same time, Darwin did a fair amount of geology, as well as detailed studies of the flora and fauna of the lands that he visited. He proved to be a bad sailor, often being dreadfully seasick. However, most of the time during the *Beagle* voyage, Darwin was not on board. He would disembark at a port and stay there or travel on land, and then rejoin the ship at a later point, when it returned after its survey up and down the coast. Darwin kept detailed diaries, which would be published in 1839 as a critically acclaimed travel book (in a later edition) titled *The Voyage of the Beagle*.

The greatest influence on Darwin during the *Beagle* voyage was the newly published (in 1830) work by the Scottish lawyer-turned-geologist, Charles Lyell. Darwin took with him the first volume of Lyell's *Principles of Geology*, and the other two subsequent volumes were sent out to him from England. Lyell was arguing for what came to be known as the "uniformitarian" view of geology. He claimed that, given enough time, all of the varied geological phenomena such as the mountains, valleys, oceans, rivers, volcanoes, and much more, can be produced by regular forces, no more intense than those presently in action—snow, rain, deposition, silting, volcanic eruptions, earthquakes, and all of the other natural effects. Darwin was impressed by this view of the Earth's history. Although his mentors at Cambridge, particularly the geologist Adam Sedgwick, had endorsed a view that came to be known as "catastrophism," where one supposes massive upheavals now and then, Darwin rejected this entirely in favor of Lyell's alternative position.

The frontispiece of the first volume of Charles Lyell's Principles of Geology published in 1830. The corrosion on the pillars, above about eight feet, suggests that after the columns had been first erected, the land sank and the pillars were submerged (and there was no corrosion beneath the surface). Then at some later point, the land rose, and the pillars emerged from their watery grave. This all supports Lyell's geological picture of Earth's history.

In fact, the first piece of scientific work that Darwin undertook, for which he is still rightfully famous, was based on Lyell's argument that the Earth is a little bit like a water bed—as one part subsides (perhaps because of silt deposits from rivers), another part rises. The major puzzle, unsolved by Lyell in the *Principles*, was that of coral reefs. Why do we find these circular, island-like phenomena in tropical seas, with coral growing around their rim? Lyell had suggested that they were the relics of now extinct volcanoes. But Darwin reasoned that it was highly unlikely that the volcanoes would have come up to, and no further than, the ocean's surface. He argued that the coral had first grown around the edges of islands, and then kept growing upwards as the islands sank. Darwin's view, incidentally, was vindicated by 20th-century science.

Lyell's uniformitarianism had two major effects on Darwin, one scientific and the other religious. On the scientific side, Lyell's insistence that geological processes are explained by regular laws of existing intensity started to push Darwin towards an evolutionary perspective on organisms, that is, the belief that organisms are naturally produced by regular laws from other forms—perhaps far more simple ones—than by miracles. Lyell himself denied evolution, but Darwin started to think otherwise. On the religious side, Lyell started Darwin on the long path that eventually led towards skepticism or agnosticism. As a young man intending to join the clergy, Darwin had been a practicing and believing Christian—a member of England's established Protestant church, the Anglican Communion. However, on the *Beagle* voyage, under Lyell's influence, Darwin increasingly found himself unable to accept religious doctrines:

> By further reflecting that the clearest evidence would be requisite to make any sane man believe in the miracles by which Christianity is supported,—that the more we know of the fixed laws of nature the more incredible do miracles become,—that the men at that time were ignorant and credulous to a degree almost incomprehensible by us,—that

the Gospels cannot be proved to have been written simultaneously with the events,—that they differ in many important details, far too important as it seemed to me to be admitted as the usual inaccuracies of eye-witnesses;—by such reflections as these, which I give not as having the least novelty or value, but as they influenced me, I gradually came to disbelieve in Christianity as a divine revelation.

It is important to emphasize that Darwin did not become an atheist, but he did start to move away from Christian "theism" to what is known as "deism"—the belief in a Supreme Being, a creator who does not intervene in the universe. This deism stayed with Darwin throughout his adult life and only towards the end did it start to fade into a form of non-belief. It goes without saying that the truth of evolution is, if anything, proof of the power of God—everything, including organism life, is produced by unbroken law without the need for intervention by the deity.

From evolution to natural selection

Darwin did not become an evolutionist on the *Beagle* voyage. However, the visit to the Galapagos Archipelago in 1835 was probably the most important event in his intellectual life. It was there that Darwin saw the giant tortoises, as well as the teeming birdlife. To his great surprise, Darwin discovered that the reptiles and the birds differed from island to island. Moreover, although they were similar to the wildlife of the South American mainland, there were also certain differences. Darwin was puzzled by these disparities. Yet, it was not until he returned to England and asked a leading authority to examine and classify his birds that Darwin made the move over to evolution. When he was told that the birds from the various islands of the Galapagos were undoubtedly different species, he could see no way of explaining this fact except through a long process of what he was to call "descent with modification."

Early in the spring of 1837, Darwin became an evolutionist. It is worth noting that, probably due to the Galapagos influence, he always thought of evolution as a branching process, starting with an original form that then diverged as the descendants got separated and went their different ways. For this reason, a branching "tree of life" was the picture of organic history adopted by Darwin and from which he never deviated. He may have made a great discovery but making it public was another matter. By this time, Darwin was starting to make a name for himself as a very promising young scientist. His work on coral reefs was gaining him much respect and he realized that "coming out" as an evolutionist would be fatal to his professional success. Therefore, although he opened some private notebooks and set out on a detailed course of inquiry, he kept his newfound belief to himself.

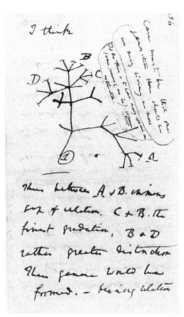

A celebrated sketch by Darwin, drawn in 1837, showing how he had grasped the idea of branching evolution.

As a graduate of the University of Cambridge, which some 200 years before housed the great Isaac Newton, Darwin realized that becoming an evolutionist was not a simple matter. As Newton had found the cause of the Copernican system–his force of gravitational attraction that exists between all bodies–so Darwin likewise realized he had to find a cause for evolution.

> Astronomers might formerly have said that God ordered each planet to move in its particular destiny. In same manner God orders each animal created with certain form in certain country. But how much more simple and sublime power,–let attraction act according to certain law, such are inevitable consequences,–let animal«s» be created, then by

the fixed laws of generation, such will be their successors. Let the powers of transportal be such, & so will be the forms of one country to another.–Let geological changes go at such a rate, so will be the number & distribution of the species!!

It took Darwin 18 months to find the solution, but he realized that the key to change lies in selection. Animal and plant breeders who wanted to produce better quality products, fatter pigs, beefier cattle, and fleshier vegetables, knew that the secret to success was picking and breeding those who, for whatever reasons, had desired characteristics. Only through this process, he postulated, could we bring about significant change. Therefore, Darwin searched for a natural equivalent to the breeders' selection. He read work after work on this topic and came across a pamphlet that drew the analogy between the world of the farmer and the natural world.

A severe winter or a scarcity of food, by destroying the weak or unhealthy, has all the good effects of the most skilful selection. In cold and barren countries no animal can live to the age of maturity, but those who have strong constitutions; the weak and the unhealthy do not live to propagate their infirmities, as is too often the case with our domestic animals. To this I attribute the peculiar hardiness of the horses, cattle, and sheep, bred in mountainous countries, more than their having been inured to the severity of climate...

Darwin took note of this passage, sensing that if this process went on long enough, we would get full-blooded species.

Sir J. Sebright–pamphlet most important showing effects of peculiarities being long in blood.++ thinks difficulty in crossing race–bad effects of incestuous intercourse.–excellent observations of sickly offspring being

cut off so that not propagated by nature.–Whole art of
making varieties may be inferred from facts stated.–

Darwin still couldn't quite make the needed, crucial move. For this,
he had to wait until the end of September 1838, when he read a work
by an Anglican clergyman, the Reverend Thomas Robert Malthus.
Malthus was interested in why human beings bothered to work at
all. Why do we not spend all our days playing and idling away the
hours? Malthus's answer was that God had made our reproductive
inclinations so strong that there is constant population pressure on
the limited availability of space and food. This leads to an inevitable
"struggle for existence." Humans, therefore, must work, and work
hard, in order to succeed; otherwise, they will starve and die.
Darwin took this Malthusian idea and applied it to the world of
animals and plants.

> Population is increase at geometrical ratio in far shorter
> time than 25 years–yet until the one sentence of Malthus no
> one clearly perceived the great check amongst men.–there
> is spring, like food used for other purposes as wheat for
> making brandy.–Even few years plenty, makes population in
> Men increase & an crop causes a dearth. take Europe on an
> average every species must have same number killed year
> with year by hawks, by cold &c.–even one species of hawk
> decreasing in number must affect instantaneously all the
> rest.–The final cause of all this wedging, must be to sort out
> proper structure, & adapt it to changes.–to do that for form,
> which Malthus shows is the final effect (by means however
> of volition) of this populousness on the energy of man. One
> may say there is a force like a hundred thousand wedges
> trying force every kind of adapted structure into the gaps in
> the oeconomy of nature, or rather forming gaps by thrusting
> out weaker ones.–

Darwin argued that for all organisms there is a constant
outstripping of food and space supplies, by ever-increasing

population numbers. Throughout nature, there is an ongoing struggle for existence, or, more precisely, struggle for reproduction. Since new variations are always appearing, (Darwin never knew why), some will succeed while others will fail in the struggle. Those that succeed will, on average, tend to be different from those, which fail. It was Darwin's great insight also to see that the differences were very important: it is precisely because organisms have different features that some succeed and others do not. Therefore, there will be an equivalent to the breeders' method of choosing, which Darwin famously labeled "natural selection."

In the course of time, natural selection will lead to change, which is evolution. It is most important to recognize that for Darwin it was never merely a matter of just "change," but change of a particular kind. Darwin thought that natural selection would lead to "adaptation:" the features of organisms would have the hand, the eye, the genitalia, the leaf, the bark, the hunting tactics of the predator, and the evasive strategies of the prey. Why was Darwin so convinced of the importance of adaptation? This was a result of the training he received at Cambridge. Part of the curriculum was the work of the Anglican clergyman Archdeacon William Paley, the author of the celebrated work *Natural Theology*, in which he gave the definitive exposition of the argument for God's design.

> In crossing a heath, suppose I pitched my foot against a *stone*, and were asked how the stone came to be there; I might possibly answer, that, for any thing I knew to the contrary, it had lain there for ever: nor would it perhaps be very easy to show the absurdity of this answer. But suppose I had found a *watch* upon the ground, and it should be inquired how the watch happened to be in that place; I should hardly think of the answer which I had before given, that, for any thing I knew, the watch might have always been there. Yet why should not this answer serve for the watch as well as for the stone? why is it not as admissible in the second case, as in the first?

Paley argued that the watch was complex in a way that did not apply to the stone: it was intricate, with many parts built to function together. Who could design it but the Creator? Continuing the argument, moving to the organic world, Paley claimed that the eye was like a telescope. Telescopes have makers and, therefore, the eye must have a maker as well: the Great Optician in the Sky. Darwin accepted completely Paley's premise, namely that the world is designed "as if." Indeed, in those early years, he did think that the organic world was designed. But whereas Paley thought that everything existed by God's design, Darwin's deistic being created through unbroken laws at a distance. The important thing is that Paley saw ubiquitous adaptation. Following Paley, Darwin saw ubiquitous adaptation brought about by natural selection.

The later years

Darwin discovered natural selection in 1838. A year or two later, he wrote a sketch of a theory based on this mechanism, and shortly thereafter a fairly detailed exposition (of 230 pages). For reasons that are not clearly understood, Darwin did not publish it. Perhaps he realized that if he were to publish his findings, he would alienate himself from powerful members of the British scientific establishment. Darwin had no desire to be a pariah. In any case, by this time he had fallen desperately sick, suffering from a combination of maladies that would leave him debilitated for the rest of his life. Early in 1839, Darwin married his first cousin Emma Wedgwood, another of Josiah Wedgwood's grandchildren. They had a conventionally large Victorian family–10 children, only seven of whom lived to majority. After the *Beagle* voyage, Darwin lived first in Cambridge, and then in London, but he needed somewhere quiet, where he could live as a semi-invalid while pursuing his studies. Thanks to family money, he and Emma were able to buy their own house in the Kentish village of Downe. There they cut themselves off from society, mainly mixing with neighbors and making extended trips to visit family members.

Darwin's illness remains a mystery to this day. Some have said that it was caused by the psychological burden of becoming an evolutionist. However, this seems unlikely because Darwin never seemed weighed down by this. Others have suggested that it was a physical ailment, Chagas disease, caused by infection from an insect bite high in the Andes during the years of the *Beagle* voyage. More recently, the suggestion has been made that Darwin suffered from lactose intolerance—an inability to digest milk products. This last hypothesis is given some credence by the fact that whenever Darwin went to health establishments, where he was put on a restricted diet, his health improved dramatically; it declined once again when he rejoined his family and started to eat the very rich diet that a comfortable middle-class family would have enjoyed on a daily basis.

Darwin slowly started to surround himself, mainly thanks to a very extensive correspondence—the Uniform Penny Post fortuitously came into being in 1840—with a group of younger scientists who would have fewer objections and prejudices to evolutionary ideas. Prominent among them were the botanist Joseph Hooker and then somewhat later the morphologist and paleontologist Thomas Henry Huxley. For many years, Darwin worked on an extensive study of barnacles. Finally, in the mid-1850s, he turned again to evolutionary studies and started writing up his work for publication.

Then, in the summer of 1858, he received from a young naturalist, out collecting in the Malay Archipelago, an essay containing virtually the same ideas that he had himself conceived 20 years previously. Spurred by the arrival of this essay written by Alfred Russel Wallace, Darwin dropped everything and wrote frenetically for 15 months. Finally, in the late fall of 1859, his seminal work, *On the Origin of Species by means of Natural Selection, or the Preservation of Favoured Races in the Struggle for Life*, was published and presented Darwin's thinking to the world.

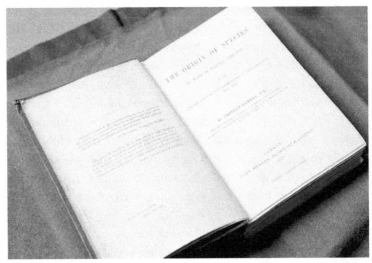

The first edition of Charles Darwin's Origin of Species.

Later in the book, we will discuss how this work had been received. Suffice it to say that, despite much controversy, the notion of evolution was quickly accepted. Natural selection, however, was a different matter. It was much criticized; but, as we will learn, the reaction was far from uniformly negative, and the full story is rather complex. Darwin himself revised the *Origin* through six editions. At the same time, he turned to other projects, including a small book on orchids, issues to do with domestication, and then, in the 1870s, an array of works on plants–insectivorous as well as climbing plants. At the beginning of that decade, he also published a major work on human evolution. *The Descent of Man and Selection in Relation to Sex* was nevertheless a rather odd book. Much of it was less about our own species and more about a secondary mechanism that Darwin had always endorsed (although hitherto not much discussed), the so-called "sexual selection." This is another matter we will take up later.

For all of the controversy, Darwin was greatly respected as a scientist. Even those whose views differed from his saw that he was a genius, whose thinking had changed our perspectives entirely and irrevocably. He was also a thoroughly nice man, who was devoted to his wife and family, a good master to his servants, a loyal friend, and one who was always ready to offer help, advice (and, if necessary, a cash gift) to those in need. When Darwin died in 1882, he was buried, by popular demand, in Westminster Abbey, alongside England's other heroes. There he lies for all eternity, next to the man whose work in physics Darwin had striven to emulate in biology: Isaac Newton.

2. Pseudoscience?

T he ancient Greeks did not believe in evolution in any sense as we would understand it. This refusal was not a matter of prejudice, religious or any other kind. It was that they did not see how a blind process of law could lead to organisms. The great philosophers Plato and Aristotle were first to realize that there was something distinctively design-like about the organic world, that adaptive nature mentioned in the previous chapter, which Darwin explained through his mechanism of natural selection. Plato believed that there was a God, who designed organisms (for that reason, his position is often spoken of as one of "external teleology"). Aristotle thought that organisms had some innate, vital force, which led to their design-like nature—the view often spoken of as "internal teleology." Either way, they both believed that organic nature precluded creation through regular law. The pre-Socratic philosopher Empedocles had argued that organisms came about randomly, through the cohesion of various parts. This is not really a full-blooded evolutionary position, but it is natural in the sense of proceeding according to blind law. Aristotle was withering in his criticism, arguing with force that such a position was ridiculous. All this demonstrates that in ancient Greece, there was no unanimous view about the origins of organisms.

The coming of Christianity did not shed more light on this matter. For many years, Christians debated about whether or not they were committed to the books of the Old Testament. After all, this was the Jewish Bible, and the Jews had rejected their Savior. Eventually, thanks to the ideas of Saint Augustine around 400 A.D., it was realized that in order to make sense of the Christian story of salvation, it was necessary to presuppose the Jewish story of creation, particularly as it involved a fall of humankind that necessitated the coming of Jesus. This meant that, with the acceptance of the process of creation that lasted six days around

6000 years ago, there were new reasons for rejecting the whole concept of evolution.

Progress

It was not until the beginning of the 18th century, a period now referred to–and for a good reason–as the Age of the Enlightenment, that we find the first stirrings of evolutionary speculation. By this time, although, by no means universally widespread, there were more and more people starting to doubt the Christian story. The corrosive effects of philosophy had done its work. Although French philosopher René Descartes was a Catholic, he had supposed the possibility of an evil demon that created false ideas for humans to believe in, including our Christian doctrine. For all that Descartes himself, as well as scores of his followers, denied that this was definitive, a seed of doubt was planted and started to grow.

Then there were the quarrels among Christians themselves. Not just the differences between Protestants and Catholics, although these were significant. There were also divergences within the Catholic community and Protestant groups as well. Indeed, in the century before, Britain had been torn apart by religious differences among Protestants. Even if one did not give up the belief in God entirely, increasingly there was space for speculation about whether any of these warring groups had a lien on the truth. Finally, voyages of exploration–particularly to Asia–had brought Europeans into contact with people who had sophisticated civilizations and religions, yet who had never heard of Jesus Christ. Could it be that Christian beliefs were just the cultural ephemera of a particular group, rather than the objective truth?

With Christianity no longer such an overwhelming force, there were stirrings of evolutionary speculation. However, the problem of design or adaptation had not been solved–this would not happen for another 150 years. In his *Critique of Judgment* (1790), German philosopher Immanuel Kant worried greatly about this problem. He did not want to bring God into science, but he could see no way of avoiding the belief–the heuristic principle if you like–that organisms seem as if they were designed. Unaided blind law was not enough. In considering a feature, we have to ask what it is for, what is its end or function, and, in finding the end or the function, we ask in a reciprocal way what brought it about, what caused it–by what means did it come into being. Kant wrote:

> An organized natural product is one in which every part is reciprocally both end and means. Such "teleological" thinking is not a luxury; it is a necessity. Life scientists "say that nothing in such forms of life is in vain, and they put the maxim on the same footing of validity as the fundamental principle of all natural science, that nothing happens by chance. They are, in fact, quite as unable to free themselves from this teleological principle as from that of general physical science. For just as the abandonment of the latter would leave them without any experience at all, so the abandonment of the former would leave them with no clue to assist their observation of a type of natural things that have once come to be thought under the conception of physical ends.

Kant was led to the rather gloomy conclusion that there would never be, as he noted in the work mentioned above, "a Newton of the blade of grass"–ultimately, he argued, the problem of adaptation was insoluble. Fortunately, others were willing to ride roughshod over these concerns. But if there was not yet a solution to adaptation, what had sparked speculations about natural origins of organisms, the belief that there was a natural development (through blind law) from very primitive to sophisticated forms? In a word, it was the ideology of *progress*. The Christian believes in Providence; that is to say that we can do nothing on our own. We are tainted, sinful and condemned to death; our only salvation lies in the blood of Jesus on the cross. Because of his great sacrifice, the possibility of eternal life is ours. That is the Christian doctrine. A believer in progress, on the other hand, claims that humans can improve their lot through education, science, civic reform, and similar activities, and, ultimately, make a good life here on earth, without God's intervention. It is interesting to note, however, that at the beginning of the 18th century, most progressivists were not atheists. Rather, they were deists. They believed that God set things in motion and then expected us to do things for ourselves. (Hence, even for the evolutionists, their laws were not entirely blind.)

These people believed that progress led directly to evolution; they also argued that there was the possibility of upwards change in the cultural realm, which also "spilled over," as it were, into the biological world. And then, equally promptly and in a circular fashion, they used biological progress to confirm their beliefs in cultural progress! You might ask why people felt progress was needed to justify their evolutionism? The simple fact is that, at the beginning of the 18th century, there was nothing else on which to rest their beliefs. The fossil record was barely uncovered; the geographical distribution of organisms across the world was hardly hinted at; discoveries in morphology and embryology had to wait another century; theories of heredity were at the crudest level. Progress, however, was a heady ideology, and its enthusiasts were ready to extend it to other fields, most particularly the domain of the living.

ERASMUS DARWIN, M.D. & F.R.S.

Engraved by McAlpin

Erasmus Darwin (1731-1802), grandfather of Charles Darwin, and in his own right a successful physician and poet.

One of the most interesting early evolutionists of the latter part of the 18th century was Darwin's grandfather, Erasmus, a British physician, inventor, agriculturalist, friend of industrialists, and popular poet. We are not quite sure what sparked his interest in evolution, although it could have been fossils that were being uncovered by laborers as they dug the channels and bored the tunnels for the canals that were starting to crisscross England. What we do know is that he believed in progress, a mindset that extended to full-blooded support of the American Revolution (he was a good friend of Benjamin Franklin). Later, he also supported the French Revolution, at least until things started to go terribly wrong in that country. The senior Darwin wrote extensively about evolution, often in poetry. As can be seen in the following 1802 poem, *The Temple of Nature*, it was always evolution with a message. It started with the blob (which, in those days, was often called the "monad") and ended with the human—the "man."

Organic life beneath the shoreless waves
Was born and nurs'd in ocean's pearly caves;
First forms minute, unseen by spheric glass,
Move on the mud, or pierce the watery mass;
These, as successive generations bloom,
New powers acquire and larger limbs assume;
Whence countless groups of vegetation spring,
And breathing realms of fin and feet and wing.

Thus the tall Oak, the giant of the wood,
Which bears Britannia's thunders on the flood;
The Whale, unmeasured monster of the main,
The lordly Lion, monarch of the plain,
The Eagle soaring in the realms of air,
Whose eye undazzled drinks the solar glare,
Imperious man, who rules the bestial crowd,
Of language, reason, and reflection proud,
With brow erect who scorns this earthy sod,
And styles himself the image of his God;
Arose from rudiments of form and sense,
An embryon point, or microscopic ens!

Erasmus' thinking was unsophisticated compared to that of his grandson Charles: in his voluminous writing, there was no systematic treatment about possible causes of evolution. There were some suggestive speculations, including an idea that was to become particularly popular in the 19th century, although less so in Charles' writings. This was the analogy between the development of the individual and the development of the group. Just as an organism grows from a speck up to the full-blooded adult, so, likewise, one supposes that the group grows from the speck to the sophisticated endpoint.

France

Many people read the poetry and prose of Erasmus Darwin. However, his influence was far eclipsed by that of the minor French nobleman, Jean-Baptiste de Lamarck. His *Philosophie Zoologique*, published in 1809 (the year of Charles Darwin's birth), had tremendous influence, if only because it was often held up as a bad example of what not to do! Lamarck became famous for the mechanism named after him, Lamarckism—the inheritance of acquired characteristics. For instance, a blacksmith gets strong arms through working in forge and, as a consequence, his son is born with strong arms, even before he starts to work. As it happens, this was only a minor part of Lamarck's thinking, and it was a mechanism already endorsed by Erasmus Darwin (and, incidentally, would also be endorsed as a secondary mechanism by Charles Darwin). Lamarck's main picture of evolution was of an upward progressive drive, starting with chemicals in ponds, which are the basis of the "spontaneous generation" of new organisms, thanks to lightning and other natural forces. Eventually, for Lamarck, as for everybody else, evolution ends with human beings.

Jean-Baptiste de Lamarck (1744-1829).

Interestingly, today we always associate evolution with a tree of life, but Lamarck did not have this picture in mind at all. He believed in parallel lines of evolution, continuing down through the ages. Organisms follow the same predetermined paths, he claimed, with occasional deviations due to the inheritance of acquired characteristics. But for someone like Darwin, an extinct species will never return, for Lamarck it is just a matter of time before it reappears in a different, parallel and upwards evolving line. Differences notwithstanding, however, Lamarck was as enthusiastic about progress as was Erasmus Darwin. If you think about it, there had to be some reason a nobleman like Lamarck not only survived the French Revolution, but also prospered during it. It was because he endorsed the philosophy behind the tumultuous events.

Unfortunately, when the Revolution went wrong and led to the dreadful events of the Terror, both in England and in France, there was a revulsion against the ideology of progress. Erasmus Darwin's thinking was savagely parodied by conservatives, including by the future Prime Minister George Canning. In the *Progress of Man*, Darwin is identified explicitly, and human bloodlust is made our defining character and woe to any unfortunate mammal that gets in our way.

> Ah, hapless porker! what can now avail,
> Thy back's stiff bristles, or thy curly tail?
> Ah! what avail those eyes so small and round,
> Long pendant ears, and snout that loves the ground?

It took many years for thoughts and hopes of societal improvement to re-emerge. Since enthusiasm for progress was that which also incited interest in evolution, in the early years of the 19th century, evolution was still a much-derided notion. This was not so much because it was regarded as anti-Christian, but it was seen as an epiphenomenon on the back of a strongly disliked ideology.

Georges Cuvier (1769-1832).

No one opposed evolution more strongly than Lamarck's fellow Frenchman, George Cuvier. He is rightly known as the father of comparative anatomy, thanks to the brilliant dissections he performed comparing and contrasting organisms of different species. He opposed evolution on many grounds, starting with the empirical. Thanks to Napoleon's expeditions to foreign lands, Egypt in particular, many specimens were brought back to Paris. These included mummies of organisms long dead. When unwrapped and dissected, Cuvier could show that the mummified forms were of species that still existed in his day. He argued, therefore, that there was no evidence of ongoing change.

Cuvier was also opposed to evolution on ideological grounds. He became a very important member of the French civil service; as such, he was deeply opposed to significant changes and looked back to the years of the Revolution with horror. Since progress led to change, he argued, then progress must be wrong, as was evolution, since it was a progressive idea. Most overwhelmingly, however, Cuvier was opposed to evolution because he was strongly committed to adaptation, the design-like nature of organisms. He had studied the works of Aristotle in great detail, and he was educated in Germany, where he fell under the sway of Kantian thinking. Cuvier could see no way in which blind law could lead to adaptation or, to use his term, to the "conditions of existence." In Cuvier's language, the conditions of existence precluded significant and ongoing development of evolution of organisms.

Britain

Cuvier articulated these ideas primarily in the second decade of the 19th century and, until Charles Darwin started publishing, for many his thinking was definitive. Cuvier was particularly influential in Great Britain, though more at the level of science and less at the level of what we might call scientific methodology. Although Cuvier was a Protestant, and therefore more likely than a Catholic to base his thinking on the Bible, he was strongly opposed to the mixing of science and religion. This belief was not shared by the British. Although by the 1820s none of the serious scientists were biblical literalists, they were all eager to see a close parallel between the science of origins and their reading of the Bible. They realized by that time that the Earth was much older than the 6000 years, as indicated in the Old Testament. But they were strongly committed to miracles, and they combined this belief with Cuvier's suggestions that there had, in fact, been upheavals in the geological past ("catastrophism"), to give a satisfying picture of origins. It was one, they thought, that combined a serious interpretation of the now rapidly growing knowledge of the fossil record, with an active and ongoing role for the creative Christian God.

Naturally, these British scientists adhered more to the side of

Providence than that of progress. However, by the 1830s, the horrors of the French Revolution were starting to recede in people's minds. At the same time, now that the Napoleonic wars were long gone, industry was starting to pick up. Therefore, thoughts of progress started to emerge once again, as did the concept of evolution. Most notably, in 1844 a Scottish publisher, Robert Chambers, who wrote anonymously, put out an evolutionary tract that rapidly became notorious for the daring nature of its speculations. *Vestiges of the Natural History of Creation* left nothing to the imagination. Starting with spontaneous generation—Chambers suggested that the frost ferns left by cold weather on windowpanes turned naturally into living plants—he saw an inevitable rise from the primitive to the complex, from the monad to the man, from the blob to the Briton. Combining a sketchy knowledge of the fossil record (most likely based on a misreading of Lamarck), with an equally cursory understanding of the then-developing Germanic studies of embryology, Chambers saw upward progress everywhere—in society, in the individual, and in the group. As he wrote in 1846:

> A progression resembling development may be traced in human nature, both in the individual and in large groups of men... Now all of this is in conformity with what we have seen of the progress of organic creation. It seems but the minute hand of a watch, of which the hour hand is the transition from species to species. Knowing what we do of that latter transition, the possibility of a decided and general retrogression of the highest species towards a meaner type is scarce admissible, but a forward movement seems anything but unlikely.

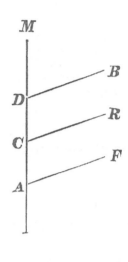

Robert Chambers (1802-1871). Alongside his portrait is a sketch from the Vestiges, supposedly showing embryological development and how prolonging it can lead to the development of higher life-forms.

Not surprisingly, Chambers' ideas were strongly condemned by the British scientific establishment. Darwin's old geology teacher at Cambridge, Adam Sedgwick, was particularly vehement, suggesting that such ridiculous ideas could only have been written by a woman; he then rescinded this view because no woman could have speculated in so vile a fashion! Yet, for all the official opposition, it is clear that many in Britain, America, and elsewhere responded favorably to Chambers' speculations. One of the most interesting, for example, was the poet Alfred Tennyson. He was writing a long poem, *In Memoriam*, dedicated to the memory of his friend, Arthur Hallam, who died young. At first, Tennyson was despondent at the seemingly meaningless message of Lyell's *Principles*–that things just keep going on and on without any progress. These are some lines from *In Memoriam*:

Are God and Nature then at strife,
That Nature lends such evil dreams?
So careful of the type she seems,
So careless of the single life;

....

So careful of the type? but no.
From scarped cliff and quarried stone
She cries, 'A thousand types are gone:
I care for nothing, all shall go

Given that Nature is "red in tooth and claw"—this is the source of this famous phrase—nothing seemed to make any sense. Not only are individuals pointless mortals, but so are whole groups. We are born, we live, and then we die—usually painfully. These are just endless Lyellian cycles.

Then Tennyson read Chambers. He found his ideas particularly inspiring, even going as far as suggesting that perhaps his dead friend was a highly evolved being who had appeared prematurely. As he wrote in *In Memoriam*:

A soul shall strike from out the vast
And strike his being into bounds,
And moved thro' life of lower phase,
Result in man, be born and think,
And act and love, a closer link
Betwixt us and the crowning race

....

Whereof the man, that with me trod
This planet, was a noble type
Appearing ere the times were ripe,
That friend of mine who lives in God.

You may feel that this is all a bit far-fetched, but remember that this is a message that Tennyson's fellow Victorians (including the Queen) found very inspiring.

By the 1850s, tucked away in the village of Downe, Darwin was still sitting on his theorizing. Although the idea of evolution was now becoming quite well known, it was still highly controversial and not at all accepted by professional scientists. It was seen, rightly, as the other side of the coin to hopes of social and cultural progress. Evolution was considered to be "pseudo," rather than mainstream science, in contrast to widely accepted fields like physics and chemistry. And this was a status very much underlined by a new arrival in the field: Herbert Spencer. Like Darwin, he was an Englishman but came from a much lower rung of the middle classes. He was not an establishment man and felt no compunction about taking on the professional scientists of his day. Completely and utterly committed to the ideology of progress, Spencer started writing at great length in favor of evolution. Interestingly and almost paradoxically, Spencer hit on the idea of natural selection, but he dismissed it as trivial. For him, it was the Lamarckian process of the inheritance of acquired characteristics that was the main cause of evolutionary change. But truly, much like Erasmus Darwin 50 years before, Spencer was less interested in causes than in ideology. It was the upward chain, whether in culture or in biology, that counted. As he wrote in *Progress: Its Law and Cause*:

> Now we propose in the first place to show, that this law of organic progress is the law of all progress. Whether it be in the development of the Earth, in the development of Life upon its surface, in the development of Society, of Government, of Manufactures, of Commerce, of Language, Literature, Science, Art, this same evolution of the simple into the complex, through successive differentiations, hold throughout. From the earliest traceable cosmical changes down to the latest results of civilization, we shall find that the transformation of the homogeneous into the heterogeneous is that in which Progress essentially consists.

Herbert Spencer (1820-1903). In the second half of the nineteenth century, Spencer was as famous as, if not more than, Charles Darwin. In the twentieth century, his reputation sank like a stone. In his Autobiography, written supposedly for private consumption, Darwin is not very complimentary about Spencer.

For Spencer, everything obeys this law. With respect to other animals, humans are more complex or heterogeneous; with respect to native people, Europeans are more complex or heterogeneous; and with respect to the tongues of other people, the English language is more complex or heterogeneous.

We see that when Darwin published the *Origin of Species* in 1859, he was not blazing completely new trails—ideas of evolution had been around for 150 years. By the middle of the 19th century, they were well known and much discussed. However, they were not respectable. It was not so much that they were considered anti-religious, although clearly there were tensions on this score—less on grounds of going against biblical literalists and more because evolution was seen as threatening to the concept of Providence—but because they were associated with a controversial ideology.

What was needed to move the story forward was a work by a reputable scientist, laying out a respectable case for evolution and its causes. This is exactly what Darwin set out to do in his seminal work, *On the Origin of Species*. In the next chapter, we will look at the pro-evolution case he made.

3. The *Origin of Species*

I n his *Autobiography*, written towards the end of his life, Charles Darwin referred to the *Origin of Species* as "one long argument." Let us take this comment seriously and explore the arguments he laid out in his seminal work.

True causes

The 1830s, when Darwin was coming to scientific maturity and making his great discovery, was a very important time in Britain for the methodology of science. Leading figures in the scientific community, most particularly the astronomer-philosopher John F.W. Herschel and the scientific polymath, historian and philosopher of science William Whewell, were articulating and specifying the framework for the best kind of science. This was not an activity done in isolation. Men like Herschel and Whewell were working hard to professionalize British science and to make full-time careers possible in the field. Therefore, it was necessary to set benchmarks against which work could be judged.

Naturally, the labors of Isaac Newton were a great inspiration. His was the best science that had ever been produced until that time, so expectedly all good science would have to emulate Newtonian characteristics. But what were those traits? Herschel and Whewell agreed that a scientific theory should be what we today call a "hypothetico-deductive system"—an axiom system, where the initial premises or axioms are law-like claims about the physical world. In the case of Newtonian mechanics, for example, we start with the three laws of motion and the law of gravitational attraction, and then we can infer Galileo's laws of motions here on Earth and Johannes Kepler's laws about the motions of planets deductively.

It was also thought that good science was causal. After all, this was the great strength of the Newtonian system: it provided an underlying cause—gravitational attraction—to explain everything. Newton himself had referred to gravity as a *vera causa* or "true cause." There was, however, some dispute about the exact nature of a true cause. Herschel, who took a somewhat empirical attitude towards science, argued that a true cause is either something that one can sense directly or something for which one has good analogical evidence. For instance, he argued that we know there is a cause pulling the Moon towards the Earth, because when we spin a stone at the end of the piece of string around our finger, we can feel the force pulling the stone towards us. Whewell, who took a somewhat rationalist attitude towards science, argued that a true cause is not necessarily something we sense but, rather, something we infer from the evidence. If it can explain a range of phenomena, which Whewell called a "consilience of inductions," then we have a true cause.

It should be noted that in the 1830s, this difference between true causes gave rise to a very lively debate. After a century of acceptance of Newton's particle theory of light, scientific opinion had swung strongly towards Huygens' wave theory. But why should one accept waves if one never sees them? Herschel offered all sorts of analogies with sound waves and water waves to provide evidence of the true-cause nature of light waves. Whewell dismissed all of this, arguing simply that light waves explain a broad range of evidence; for that reason alone, they should be accepted as a true cause. Geology was also raised in the debate. Herschel argued that Lyellian uniformitarianism, specifying, as it did, that the past should be explained in terms of causes of the present, satisfied the empiricists' true-cause criteria. Whewell argued that catastrophism was a perfectly acceptable geological position. If, for instance, there are geological phenomena, like mountain ranges, that demand the supposition of forces that we do not experience today, then it is acceptable to suppose them in order to get a full explanation. In other words, we have a true cause.

Artificial selection

Darwin had known Whewell when he was an undergraduate and spent much time with him in the early years after the *Beagle* voyage. He read Whewell's writings carefully. Darwin had also read Herschel's little book on scientific methodology just before he left on the *Beagle*. He then met with Herschel when the ship docked in South Africa, where Herschel was spending several years mapping the heavens of the southern hemisphere. This is to say that Darwin was familiar with the positions of these two men. Eager to provide a theory that was methodologically sound, he covered his options by trying to satisfy both the Herschelian empiricist demands for a true cause and the Whewellian rationalist demands for a true cause. He left nothing to chance.

Darwin opened the *Origin* with a detailed discussion of selection as practiced by animal and plant breeders:

> Altogether at least a score of pigeons might be chosen, which, if shown to an ornithologist, and he were told that they were wild birds, would certainly, I think, be ranked by him as well-defined species. Moreover, I do not believe that any ornithologist would place the English carrier, the short-faced tumbler, the runt, the barb, pouter, and fantail in the same genus; more especially as in each of these breeds several truly inherited sub-breeds, or species as he might have called them, could be shown him.
>
> Great as the differences are between the breeds of pigeons, I am fully convinced that the common opinion of naturalists is correct, namely, that all have descended from the rock-pigeon (Columba livia), including under this term several geographical races or sub-species, which differ from each other in the most trifling respects.

In part, Darwin was clearly using this information heuristically to lead the reader towards the main claims of his theory. He felt that if the reader could understand what happened in the world of the breeder, then claims about natural selection and its evolutionary implications would be more readily grasped. However, Darwin was also preparing the way to use human selection as a form of support for natural selection. He was arguing that the great successes breeders achieved, for instance with pigeons, mirrored the results yielded by natural processes used with wild animals and plants. In other words, the discussion of artificial selection was intended as a Herschelian, empiricist true cause. We have an analogy between something that we can see and work on ourselves and something that is not directly observable and must in some sense be inferred.

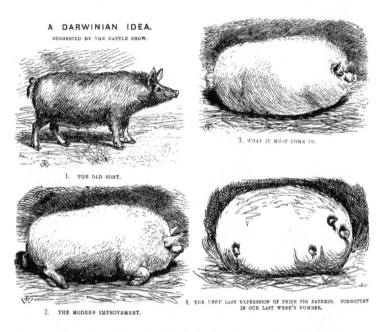

A humorous account of how artificial selection changes the wild pig into something fit for human use.

Incidentally, Darwin always presupposed that natural selection would be a rather slow process. He never really envisioned the possibility that we might see natural selection actually taking place and having effects in our lifetime.

Natural selection

Next in the *Origin*, Darwin went on to introduce his chief mechanism of change. He noted that nothing was possible without a constant supply of new variation. Darwin never had an adequate theory of heredity; but he was always fully convinced that, whatever the causes, any natural population of organisms would show considerable variation and that new variations would appear from one generation to another. Likewise, he was always adamant that these variations would never be directed towards an organism's needs. They were, he argued, completely random; not in the sense of being uncaused—even though Darwin knew nothing about the causes, he was convinced that such causes existed—but in the sense that they did not occur according to need.

Then, with the variation, Darwin was ready to introduce first the idea of the struggle for existence, and then the notion of natural selection. About the struggle, he wrote as follows:

> A struggle for existence inevitably follows from the high rate at which all organic beings tend to increase. Every being, which during its natural lifetime produces several eggs or seeds, must suffer destruction during some period of its life, and during some season or occasional year, otherwise, on the principle of geometrical increase, its numbers would quickly become so inordinately great that no country could support the product. Hence, as more individuals are produced than can possibly survive, there must in every case be a struggle for existence, either one individual with another of the same species, or with the individuals of

distinct species, or with the physical conditions of life. It is the doctrine of Malthus applied with manifold force to the whole animal and vegetable kingdoms; for in this case there can be no artificial increase of food, and no prudential restraint from marriage.

Then, Darwin went on to infer natural selection:

Let it be borne in mind in what an endless number of strange peculiarities our domestic productions, and, in a lesser degree, those under nature, vary; and how strong the hereditary tendency is. Under domestication, it may be truly said that the whole organization becomes in some degree plastic. Let it be borne in mind how infinitely complex and close-fitting are the mutual relations of all organic beings to each other and to their physical conditions of life. Can it, then, be thought improbable, seeing that variations useful to man have undoubtedly occurred, that other variations useful in some way to each being in the great and complex battle of life, should sometimes occur in the course of thousands of generations? If such do occur, can we doubt (remembering that many more individuals are born than can possibly survive) that individuals having any advantage, however slight, over others, would have the best chance of surviving and of procreating their kind? On the other hand we may feel sure that any variation in the least degree injurious would be rigidly destroyed. This preservation of favourable variations and the rejection of injurious variations, I call Natural Selection.

Although these arguments are rather informal, Darwin was clearly intending some kind of hypothetical-deductive picture. We start with laws—for instance about the tendency of organisms to increase in number geometrically and the impossibility of food and space supplies to ever match this tendency. We then go on to infer the struggle for existence. After this, we include a premise about the existence of variation in all populations, combine it with the conclusion about struggle, and go on to deduce natural selection. Nothing is very rigorous, but the intention is clear.

Geospiza magnirostris

"Darwin's finches." These birds were drawn from life on the Beagle voyage and have since been named after the great naturalist. The important point to note is their very strong beaks. These are "adaptations" produced by natural selection for eating nuts and other tough foodstuffs. Other species of finch have very fine beaks, good for eating seeds and other delicate morsels. There are even a couple of species of finch that are tool users, picking up twigs in their beaks and poking around in the bark of trees for insects.

Along with natural selection, Darwin also introduced the secondary mechanism of sexual selection. Clearly influenced by practices in the breeders' world, Darwin divided sexual selection—resulting from competition between organisms of the same species for mates—into two kinds. First, there is sexual selection because of the "male combat," occurring when males compete for mates, as when two stags fight over the female herd. It leads to such physical characteristics as antlers and is obviously modeled on the results of breeders selecting more ferocious fighting dogs or cockerels. The second sexual selection is done by female species—they choose what they regard as the most desirable male. It leads to physical characteristics like the stupendous tail feathers of the male peacock and is obviously modeled on the results of breeders selecting for melodious songbirds, and so forth.

Darwin also introduced what he called his "principle of divergence"—the process whereby organisms differentiate into new groups or species (meaning populations that are reproductively isolated from all other organisms). This process occurs, Darwin argued, because greater differentiation means greater opportunities to exploit the environment. If everything is exactly the same, then everyone is competing against everyone else. However, with differentiation, different organisms can exploit diverging ecological niches. This leads to the tree of life. Darwin wrote:

> The affinities of all the beings of the same class have sometimes been represented by a great tree. I believe this simile largely speaks the truth. The green and budding twigs may represent existing species; and those produced during each former year may represent the long succession of extinct species.

In fact, the only illustration given in the *Origin* to back up the discussion of the principle of divergence is of the tree "As buds give rise by growth to fresh buds, and these, if vigorous, branch out and overtop on all sides many a feebler branch, so by generation I believe it has been with the great Tree of Life, which fills with its dead and broken branches the crust of the earth, and covers the surface with its ever branching and beautiful ramifications."

Consilience

With the main mechanism now introduced, Darwin quickly covered some of the difficulties in his theory—most particularly, he acknowledged his ignorance about the true causes of heredity. Then, he was ready to apply the mechanism and found Whewell's influence to be paramount. Darwin wanted to incorporate natural selection in a consilience of inductions, showing it to be a true cause because it could explain different phenomena right through the spectrum of the life sciences. This was his project for the second half of the *Origin of Species.*

Darwin started with social behavior, most particularly focusing on the Hymenoptera, ants, bees, and wasps. He always recognized that behavior was as important in the struggle for existence as any physical feature, so, in essence, selection worked to promote adaptive behaviors. Generally, this is of no great significance. The wolf becomes faster in order to catch the prey; the rabbit gets quicker or better at maneuvering to avoid the predator. However, Darwin noticed that in social animals, behavior started to raise an interesting and difficult problem. For instance, one animal will put much effort into promoting the well-being of another animal, just like the workers in the hive devote all of their energies to the well-being of the queen and her offspring. Darwin always interpreted the struggle as being one organism against another; therefore, he could not immediately see how selection could produce what we today call "altruism."

A bee hive. One of the strengths of Darwin's writings was the way in which he skillfully used illustrations that would be familiar to his readers. Many people in the nineteenth century, especially in more rural areas, kept a hive or two of bees.

Hampered by the lack of an adequate theory of heredity, Darwin had problems on this issue. He could see why the behavior of social insects was adaptive. For instance, he went to considerable trouble to show that the hexagonal form of the honeycomb was by far the most efficient use of the wax. In other words, he showed that adaptation could extend itself from the organism to the objects the organism produces. (This is what the English biologist Richard Dawkins has called an "extended phenotype.") But Darwin was baffled by the behavior that served the aims of others. One thing that he was adamant about was that one could never simply have an organism working for the good of another, without some kind of reciprocity. Eventually, Darwin decided that in some way it was appropriate to consider the group—such as the nest or the hive—as one interrelated individual. Therefore, we should look upon the sterile worker—who is always female—less as an individual in her own right, and more as a part of the whole. Just as the human heart, lungs, and brain all work together for the benefit of the individual, so do hive workers serve the cause of their community.

Darwin then went on to discuss paleontology. You might think that this would be the easiest area of all for an evolutionist to tackle. However, Darwin did not see it this way. He was very much aware of such problems as gaps in the fossil record and knew that critics of evolution had seized on this as evidence that later forms (fossils found higher in the record) were not descended from earlier forms (fossils found lower in the record). He devoted much time and effort to arguing that gaps in the fossil record were truly artifactual: either they represented points of which we had incomplete knowledge but linking fossils would be found later, or they represented points where we had incomplete knowledge, but the gaps would never be filled because the needed fossilization never occurred. Either way, it was more reasonable to suppose that the gaps were inadequacies in the record, rather than a faithful reflection of what actually happened.

Obviously, paleontology was not just a matter of explaining deficiencies and problems. Going on the offensive, Darwin made much of the fact that there was a fairly well-articulated progress in the record from more primitive to the complex forms we still have around us today. More than this, he pointed out that earlier forms were often more generalized, having features that are today shared by very different organisms. Darwin also theorized that the earlier, generalized forms were the shared ancestors of the later diverse organisms. He was aware that the early generalized forms were often similar to the embryos of later forms. However, he never endorsed a simple picture of organisms going from the embryonic to the adult, in geological time as well as in individual time. Apart from anything else, this would seem to imply a kind of inevitable momentum to the course of evolutionary history. Darwin always thought that evolution, fueled as it was by natural selection, was a much more contingent and random phenomena, which offered no guarantee that one form will necessarily lead to another.

Next, Darwin turned to geographical distributions of organisms. Expectedly, given that this was the area that had first sparked his evolutionary inclinations—the reptiles and birds of the Galapagos Archipelago—Darwin felt very much at home here, arguing strongly that one could explain distributions only on the evolutionary basis. One thing he particularly stressed was the fact that the inhabitants of oceanic islands were almost always much closer in form to the inhabitants of the nearest continental mainland than to mainlands elsewhere. The Galapagos organisms, for example, looked like South American organisms and not at all like African organisms. Conversely, the organisms of the Canary Islands in the Atlantic, close to the coast of Africa, had a definite African tinge, rather than resembling inhabitants of South America.

From here, Darwin went on to look at systematics. It was in the 18th century that, thanks to the Swedish biologist Carl Linnaeus, a proper order was imposed on the wide range of animals and plants to be found on Earth. Among biologists concerned with classification, there was considerable debate about which criteria lead to natural or objective systems and which lead to artificial or subjective systems. However, by the middle of the 19th century, people were starting to get a real sense of truly natural orderings, as opposed to just conveniences imposed on the organic world by the classifier. For instance, no one was about to deny that the sea mammals like whales should be classified with other mammals rather than with fish, or that flightless birds like the ostrich or emu belonged with other birds and not with the mammals. Darwin proudly pointed out that there was a good reason for taking this classification as uniquely natural: it represented the course of history. Whales were descended from other mammals and only at a distance from fish. The ostrich and the emu originated from other birds and not from mammals. Evolution through natural selection was the key to natural classification.

Next came morphology or anatomy. It had been known since Aristotle that there were isomorphisms—similarities in organisms of different ancestry—among the bones of different organisms. The forelimb of the horse, the human, the seal, the mole—not to mention the wings of bats and birds—seem as if modeled on the same plan, even though the functions are different. Why should this be so? Was it simply that God somewhat capriciously decided to work from one pattern and mold everything accordingly? It was Darwin's argument that the similarities, now known as "homologies," were the result of evolution through selection. There was the ancestral, rather general form, and then through the ages selection turned the individual organisms to their different ends. One has a nice combination of what was traditionally known as "unity of type," meaning similarity of form, with "conditions of existence"—the difference of function.

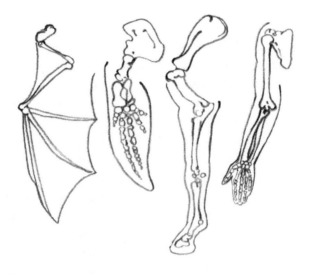

The homologies between the forelimbs of vertebrates of different species.

In fact, Darwin had already made a more general point when he was earlier discussing apparent difficulties on his theory.

> It is generally acknowledged that all organic beings have been formed on two great laws—Unity of Type, and the Conditions of Existence. By unity of type is meant that fundamental agreement in structure, which we see in organic beings of the same class, and which is quite independent of their habits of life. On my theory, unity of type is explained by unity of descent. The expression of conditions of existence, so often insisted on by the illustrious Cuvier, is fully embraced by the principle of natural selection. For natural selection acts by either now adapting the varying parts of each being to its organic and inorganic conditions of life; or by having adapted them during long-past periods of time: the adaptations being

aided in some cases by use and disuse, being slightly affected by the direct action of the external conditions of life, and being in all cases subjected to the several laws of growth. Hence, in fact, the law of the Conditions of Existence is the higher law; as it includes, through the inheritance of former adaptations, that of Unity of Type.

Towards the end, Darwin turned with some pleasure to embryology. The German biologists, particularly Karl Ernst von Baer, had shown significant similarities between the embryos of organisms that were very different as adults, the human and the chick, for example. Why should this be so? Darwin argued simply that it represented shared ancestry. Natural selection did not tear the embryos apart because they were protected in the womb or the egg. Selection, however, did work on the adults. At this point, Darwin made use of his Herschelian vera causa argument, showing that very similar phenomena could be found in the world of the animal breeder: horse and dog breeders cared about the adults, not the young. Darwin found that, expectedly, the young of bulldogs and greyhounds were much more similar than the adults. Likewise, the young of cart horses and racehorses shared more similarities than the adults. This was a fitting confirmation of Darwin's position, especially since the breeders themselves had denied that this was so! He wrote:

> Some authors who have written on Dogs, maintain that the greyhound and bulldog, though appearing so different, are really varieties most closely allied, and have probably descended from the same wild stock; hence I was curious to see how far their puppies differed from each other: I was told by breeders that they differed just as much as their parents, and this, judging by the eye, seemed almost to be the case; but on actually measuring the old dogs and their six-days old puppies, I found that the puppies had not nearly acquired their full amount of proportional difference. So, again, I was told that the foals of cart and race-horses

differed as much as the full-grown animals; and this surprised me greatly, as I think it probable that the difference between these two breeds has been wholly caused by selection under domestication; but having had careful measurements made of the dam and of a three-days old colt of a race and heavy cart-horse, I find that the colts have by no means acquired their full amount of proportional difference.

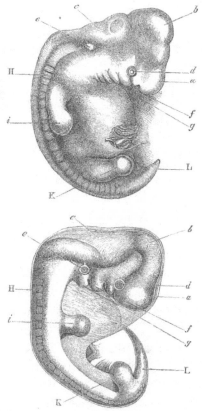

Fig. 1. Upper figure human embryo, from Ecker. Lower figure that of a dog, from Bischoff.

---

a. Fore-brain, cerebral hemispheres, &c.
b. Mid-brain, corpora quadrigemina.
c. Hind-brain, cerebellum, medulla oblongata.
d. Eye.
e. Ear.
f. First visceral arch.

g. Second visceral arch.
H. Vertebral columns and muscles in process of development.
i. Anterior ⎱ extremities.
K. Posterior ⎰
L. Tail or os coccyx.

The embryo of a human (above) and a dog (below).

The consilience was completed. Darwin had shown the evolution through natural selection across the spectrum of the life sciences. Conversely, the explanations point to the truth of the Darwinian true cause, natural selection. Darwin wrote:

> It is interesting to contemplate an entangled bank, clothed with many plants of many kinds, with birds singing on the bushes, with various insects flitting about, and with worms crawling through the damp earth, and to reflect that these elaborately constructed forms, so different from each other, and dependent upon each other, in so complex a manner, have all been produced by laws acting around us. These laws, taken in the largest sense, being Growth with Reproduction... a Rate of Increase so high as to lead to a Struggle for Life, and as a consequence Natural Selection entailing, a Divergence of Character and the extinction of less-improved forms. Thus, from the war of nature, from famine and death, the most exalted object we are capable of conceiving, namely, the production of the higher animals, directly follows. There is grandeur in this view of life, with its several powers, having been originally breathed into a few forms or into one; and that, whilst this planet has gone cycling on according to the fixed law of gravity, from so simple a beginning endless forms most beautiful and most wonderful have been and are being, evolved.

In the next chapter, we will discuss the response to Darwin's findings.

4. Reception

J ohn Murray, Charles Darwin's publisher, printed 1250 copies of the *Origin of Species*. Darwin was worried that many would be left over, but Murray knew better. On the first day of his half-yearly sale of books to booksellers, the *Origin* sold out completely. Darwin was ordered to start preparing the second edition. It was as if the world had been waiting for this particular book. At the time, evolution was a much-discussed and highly controversial idea; what was needed was a definitive work by a major scientist. The *Origin* fulfilled that need.

The fact of evolution

Evolution was, as mentioned above, a contentious concept. Famous, even today, was the clash between Thomas Henry Huxley, representing the side of science, and Bishop Samuel Wilberforce of Oxford, speaking out for religion. In the summer of 1860, they debated at the annual meeting of the British Association for the Advancement of Science at Oxford. Supposedly, Wilberforce asked Huxley if he was descended from monkeys on his grandfather or grandmother's side. Huxley reportedly responded that he would rather be descended from a monkey than from a Bishop of the Church of England! The story is almost surely apocryphal, but even myths tell truths. Darwin's theory of evolution through natural selection did cause a major upheaval in Victorian Britain, and the dispute did lead to one of the most enjoyable squibs in English literature. Rapidly, the conflict between Huxley and the scientist who coached Wilberforce, the anatomist Richard Owen, crystallized into a fight over the nature of the human brain. Did it uniquely have the hippocampus minor, as was claimed by Owen, or was the hippocampus minor also found in the brains of the higher apes, as was Huxley suggested? The clergyman (and ardent evolutionist) Charles Kingsley took up the issue, and in his *Water-Babies* made much fun of the quarrel:

> Now it befell that, on the very shore, and over the very rocks, where Tom was sitting with his friend the lobster, there walked one day the little white lady, Ellie herself, and with her a very wise man indeed – Professor Ptthmllnsprts... He held very strange theories about a good many things. He had even got up once at the British Association, and declared that apes had hippopotamus majors in their brains just as men have. Which was a shocking thing to say; for, if it were so, what would become of the faith, hope, and charity of immortal millions? You may think that there are other more important differences between you and an ape, such as being able to speak, and make machines, and know right from wrong, and say your prayers, and other little matters of that kind; but that is a child's fancy, my dear. Nothing is to be depended on but the great hippopotamus test. If you have a hippopotamus major in your brain, you are no ape, though you had four hands, no feet, and were more apish than the apes of all aperies. But if a hippopotamus major is ever discovered in one single ape's brain, nothing will save your great-great-great-great-great-great-great-great-great-great-great-greater-greatest-grandmother   from having been an ape too.

A cartoon of Thomas Henry Huxley (1825-1895). Note how he is dressed in a modern suit, as befits a forward-looking scientist. He was known as "Darwin's Bulldog."

A cartoon of Samuel Wilberforce, Bishop of Oxford (1805-1873). Note how he is dressed in the Elizabethan garb of a bishop, showing that he harks back through the centuries. He was known as "Soapy Sam," because of his somewhat unctuous mannerisms. He was a son of William Wilberforce, the great opponent of slavery.

Joking apart—or perhaps because of the jokes—most people very quickly accepted the fact of evolution. It became almost commonsensical. Darwin had accumulated so much evidence that it became difficult to deny that organisms had emerged slowly and gradually by natural processes. In 1866, the examinations for students at the University of Cambridge even went so far as to say that the truth of evolution should be assumed, and examinees should focus on discussion of causes. In one of his early novels, A *Pair of Blue Eyes* published in 1873, English novelist Thomas Hardy had one of his characters stuck half way up a cliff and afraid of falling. As is customary on these occasions, Hardy had the history of life pass before the unfortunate fellow's eyes; however, the clever twist—spurred by the recognition of a trilobite embedded in the cliff to which he was clinging—did not unfurl the poor chap's life but, rather, the history of life in general.

> Time closed up like a fan before him. He saw himself at one extremity of the years, face to face with the beginning and all the intermediate centuries simultaneously. Fierce men, clothed in the hides of beasts, and carrying, for defence and attack, huge clubs and pointed spears, rose from the rock, like the phantoms before the doomed Macbeth. They lived in hollows, woods, and mud huts—perhaps in caves of the neighbouring rocks. Behind them stood an earlier band. No man was there. Huge elephantine forms, the mastodon, the hippopotamus, the tapir, antelopes of monstrous size, the megatherium, and the myledon—all, for the moment, in juxtaposition. Further back, and overlapped by these, were perched huge-billed birds and swinish creatures as large as horses. Still more shadowy were the sinister crocodilian outlines— alligators and other uncouth shapes, culminating in the colossal lizard, the iguanodon. Folded behind were dragon forms and clouds of flying reptiles: still underneath were fishy beings of lower development; and so on, till the lifetime scenes of the fossil confronting him were a present and modern condition of things.

Natural selection

What about Darwin's mechanism of natural selection? We need to step carefully here. As mentioned in Chapter One, in one sense or dimension the fate of natural selection was very different from the reception of the fact of evolution. No one wanted to deny its existence completely. However, among those with pretensions to scientific competence—and note this important qualification—there were few who wanted to give it the importance that Darwin proposed in the *Origin*. For example, although Huxley was happy to debate evolution with everybody and anybody, as a scientist he never was much of an enthusiast for natural selection. To the contrary, he thought that now and then there were jumps—the so-called "saltations"—taking organisms from one form to another, in just one generation. Others continued to stress the importance of Lamarckism, the inheritance of acquired characteristics. We have seen that Herbert Spencer fell into this category. A third group wanted to put some God-driven guidance into the new variations. Asa Gray, the professor of botany at Harvard University, and Darwin's great North American supporter was one who thought this way. And we find another group, often inspired by Germanic thinking, which thought that there was a kind of momentum to evolution, driving it ever upwards. These were the people who were particularly keen on analogies between the development of the individual and the development of the group. Most famous was the German morphologist Ernst Haeckel, who incorporated these ideas into his famous "biogenetic law:" "ontogeny recapitulates phylogeny."

Why was there rejection of natural selection? In part, this came about in a negative sort of way. Darwin thought that the most important characteristic of the organic world was the way in which features are so very adapted to the needs of their possessors; natural selection was promoted to explain this fact. However, by the 1850s, biologists were far less impressed with adaptation. They had moved away from naturalistic studies of organisms in the wild, the sorts of things that Darwin was looking at when he was in South America during the *Beagle* voyage, to laboratory studies of dead organisms on the dissecting table. The big questions in the 1850s centered on homology and structure, that is to say, Unity of Type. Questions of design and success in life—those relating to Conditions of Existence—were regarded to be relatively unimportant. So in a sense, by the time the *Origin* was published in 1859, many thought that natural selection was a solution to a non-existent problem.

In part, the rejection of natural selection came about in a positive sort of way, meaning that actual arguments were brought against it. In the scientific world particularly, many thought that there were insuperable difficulties to its acceptance. For a start, as has been pointed out earlier, Darwin had no adequate theory of heredity. Without this, natural selection was always vulnerable. If you cannot show why new variations will be passed on from generation to generation without being diluted, then no matter how effective selection may be, there's always the danger that it will fade away in two or three generations. This was the objection of the Scottish engineer Fleeming Jenkin. Even Darwin himself thought Jenkin made a good point.

There was an even bigger obstacle in the way of natural selection. The physicists had devised various ways of calculating the age of the Earth. They were based on such factors as the heat received on Earth from the Sun; the saltiness of the sea; the heat expected from the Earth's core based on increasing temperatures as one goes deeper and deeper into mines; and other such phenomena. The general estimate was that the Earth could not be more than 400 million years old and that it could be as young as 25 million years. The favored middle figure was about 100 million years. But this was felt by many scientists to be far too short a time for such an allegedly slow process like natural selection. Hence, other mechanisms would be needed.

Of course, today we know that the physicists were wildly inaccurate in their calculations. They were ignorant of the warming effects of radioactive decay. Nowadays we believe that the universe as a whole is just under 14 billion years old, and that the Earth is about 4.5 billion years old. The earlier life seems to have appeared about 3.75 billion years ago. At the time of the *Origin*, however, this was unknown, and this void in knowledge was a major impediment to the acceptance of natural selection.

Darwin was convinced that he was right. Interestingly, whenever he was challenged on selection, he invoked the example of the wave theory of light, arguing that since this concept was accepted, selection should be accepted on the same grounds. Also, at every opportunity, he seized on new, favorable information. For instance, early in the 1860s in Germany, the first specimens of Archaeopteryx, the transitional fossil between the birds and reptiles, were discovered. Darwin introduced this organism into one of the later editions of the *Origin*, trumpeting it as proof that gaps in the fossil record were a function of ignorance rather than genuine absence. Around the same time, a young naturalist and sometime traveling companion of Alfred Russel Wallace came up with a very ingenious, selection-based explanation of the mimicry among different species of butterflies. English naturalist and explorer Henry Walter Bates argued that some butterflies were naturally poisonous and, therefore, had an adaptation against their predators, the birds. Other butterflies had no poisonous taste but had found it advantageous to mimic their toxic counterparts. In a series of ingenious experiments, Bates showed how one could reasonably infer that this was the result of a selective process. Darwin was very excited by this explanation, and it found its way into a later edition of the *Origin*. However, somewhat curiously—and in line with what has been said earlier about Darwin's never believing that selection could actually be seen in action—he relegated Bates' explanation to a secondary position at the end of the book. One might have thought that it would have been introduced early and made prize specimen in the evidential gallery.

ILLUSTRATIONS OF MIMICRY BETWEEN BUTTERFLIES.
(Reproduced from Plate 55, Trans. Linn. Soc. XXIII. Pt. 3)
by kind permission of the Linnean Society.

1.—Leptalis Theonoë.   *2.—Leptalis Theonoë, var. Melanoë.*   *3.—Leptalis Theonoë, var. Lysinoë.*

1a.—Ithomia Flora.   *2a.—Ithomia Onega.*   *3a.—Stalachtis Phædusa.*

Batesian mimicry. The butterflies in the top row are the mimics of the butterflies, the models, in the bottom row. The top-row butterflies are quite palatable to birds, but are avoided because birds mistakenly think that they are bottom-row butterflies that are quite foul tasting.

Initial conclusion

It seems that, thus far, the Darwinian story had only a very limited success. True, people now accepted the fact of evolution. But Darwin, though he rushed to introduce this idea, was not the first to propose it; by the 1860s, more and more people were toying with this theory. When it came to mechanisms—avoiding the error now known as Whiggism of judging everything in the light of our knowledge today—Darwin's thinking was really a bit of a flop. He did not make the most use of what materials he had at hand, and others—his friends and supporters—generally were less enthused about natural selection. Little wonder that one prominent historian of science (Peter Bowler) has written a well-regarded work on the non-Darwinian Revolution, and recently he has followed it with a counter-history, arguing that if Darwin never existed, today we would still be in much the same place as we are. He is not alone, and his position is not unusual. Yet, while the general facts cannot be denied—I gave them myself in an overview history of the Darwinian revolution written over three decades ago—to leave matters here would be distorting almost to the point of perversion. But to see this, we have to look at the broader, cultural context. First, however, we need to introduce the all-important factor—humankind.

In the next chapter, we will look at what Darwin had to say about human beings and then go on to explore the implications and ramifications of these ideas.

5. The *Descent of Man*

I n the *Origin*, Darwin said very little about humankind. Before all discussion was swamped by a tsunami of controversy about human origins, he wanted to get the basic principles of his theory out in public. Hence, he made only a throwaway comment at the end, about the significance of his theory for our own species. He did this so as not to be accused of cowardice on the subject. He wrote:

> In the distant future I see open fields for far more important researches. Psychology will be based on a new foundation, that of the necessary acquirement of each mental power and capacity by gradation. Light will be thrown on the origin of man and his history.

Reticence, however, should not be confused with hesitation. There was no doubt in Darwin's mind about the applicability of his theory to *Homo sapiens*. Interestingly, in one of his private evolution notebooks for 1838, the very first mention we have of natural selection in action is a speculation about how the human brain will grow under the actions of this mechanism:

> An habitual action must some way affect the brain in a manner which can be transmitted.–this is analogous to a blacksmith having children with strong arms.–The other principle of those children, which chance? produced with strong arms, outliving the weaker ones, may be applicable to the formation of instincts, independently of habits.

Darwin was always convinced that humans are part of the natural order of things. This fit in nicely with his deistic beliefs and probably was connected to his experiences on the *Beagle* voyage. On a previous trip, the captain of the *Beagle*, Robert FitzRoy, had brought back to England four of the natives of the southernmost tip of South America, the already-mentioned Tierra del Fuego. One died, and the others were being returned to their homeland on the voyage that Darwin took. When they were put ashore, within a week or two, to the horrified amazement of the Beagle's crew these natives reverted quickly back to what the Victorians called "savages." It convinced the ship's naturalist that human nature was very close to that of an animal. He learned a lesson that he never forgot. Darwin's horrified feelings come through strongly in the account he was to write of the *Beagle* voyage.

Tierra del Fuegians depicted by the artist on board HMS Beagle.

At a subsequent period the Beagle anchored for a couple of days under Wollaston Island, which is a short way to the northward. While going on shore we pulled alongside a canoe with six Fuegians. These were the most abject and miserable creatures I any where beheld.... [T]hese Fuegians in the canoe were quite naked, and even one full-grown woman was absolutely so. It was raining heavily, and the fresh water, together with the spray, trickled down her body. In another harbour not far distant, a woman, who was suckling a recently-born child, came one day alongside the vessel, and remained there whilst the sleet fell and thawed on her naked bosom, and on the skin of her naked child. These poor wretches were stunted in their growth, their hideous faces bedaubed with white paint, their skins filthy and greasy, their hair entangled, their voices discordant, their gestures violent and without dignity. Viewing such men, one can hardly make oneself believe they are fellow-creatures, and inhabitants of the same world.

Darwin was reticent on the subject of human origins; others were far less cautious. Thomas Henry Huxley, in particular, was pushing a materialist philosophy and made the natural origins of humankind a major plank in his world picture. He wrote a little book, *Man's Place in Nature*, arguing strongly for our animal nature. Others did much the same. Although Darwin was responsible for one of the biggest controversies of his age, he always shrank back from violent confrontations. He preferred to tend to his illnesses in the security of his family, tucked away in the Kentish countryside. Probably, he would have been happy to let others carry on the discussion about humankind. However, it was not to be. Alfred Russel Wallace, the co-discoverer of natural selection, spent the 1860s becoming more and more enthusiastic about spiritualism. Finally, he took to arguing that humankind could only have come about thanks to the intervention and guidance of spirit forces. In other words, Wallace gave up entirely on a naturalistic explanation of our origins.

Alfred Russel Wallace (1823-1913). From the lowest levels of the middle classes, Wallace was a total contrast to Darwin, being always in chase of some wild hypothesis that brought him scorn from the secure and successful. Indifferent to status, Wallace always generously acknowledged Darwin's supremacy and despite their differences, there was friendship and respect.

Darwin was appalled. He thought, with good reason, that Wallace was doing his best to destroy the credibility of natural selection. Something had to be done, but what? The trouble was that spiritualism or not, Wallace brought forward some good arguments against the all-conquering power of natural selection. In particular, he pointed out that many human characteristics almost certainly did not come into being thanks to natural selection. Human hair was one example, and human intelligence was another. Although Darwin had seen many natives during his years in and around South America, he had never lived with them. But Wallace had done just that. He had spent some four or five years in South America collecting butterflies, and then a year or two later he went east to the Malay Archipelago, where he spent, even more, time.

Without Darwin's unlimited funds, Wallace had to live in a relatively simple way. This meant sharing accommodations with the native people he encountered. Wallace was impressed by the way natives obviously underutilized their potential brainpower. Although he was sure that native people could be as intellectually developed as Europeans, in reality, this rarely happened. As Wallace pointed out, it seemed that for many years humans had a huge amount of unused brain capacity. This could hardly have been brought about by natural selection because having a brain is clearly biologically costly. Proto-humans could not have afforded such a luxury, at least not on naturalistic grounds. There had to be a reason. Wallace's conclusion was that spirit forces prepared the brain's early form, which waited to be used when European civilization got underway.

The Descent of Man

At this point, Darwin turned for help to sexual selection, which explained the already-mentioned rather odd balance on humankind in the *Descent of Man*. Darwin argued that many human characteristics were indeed inexplicable on natural selection; however, they could be readily explained thanks to sexual selection. In particular, Darwin argued that human intelligence could have emerged through a struggle for mates, whether through combat of males or the selection of females of the men that they preferred. To be frank, one rather feels that Darwin got carried away by this topic. He discussed sexual selection in the *Descent* very much in its own right and at great length. However, the overall intent was to develop and present a secondary mechanism, something that could then explain important aspects of human nature.

The *Descent* appeared in 1871. It was not, and did not pretend to be, a work of the same staggering originality as the *Origin of Species*. By the time Darwin was writing the *Descent*, there had been a decade of inquiry and speculation about human nature and its evolutionary origins. Darwin, therefore, was able to draw extensively on the work of others. Nevertheless, the book could only have been written by the author of the *Origin*. Darwin gave a very detailed exposition of the path of human origins as best known at the time. He also tried to show how natural selection could account for the main aspects of our evolution. Although Darwin was to make much of sexual selection in explaining human evolution, he never doubted that natural selection overall was the main force of change.

Expectedly, given the *Origin*'s fascination with social evolution in the insects, the *Descent* devoted considerable attention to questions of social evolution in humankind. Darwin was particularly keen to show that our moral sense comes naturally and does not demand a supernatural explanation. For a start, he argued that morality could well have come through what is today known as "reciprocal altruism"—you scratch my back, and I'll scratch yours. This is how Darwin phrased this concept:

> In the first place, as the reasoning powers and foresight of the members became improved, each man would soon learn that if he aided his fellow-men, he would commonly receive aid in return. From this low motive he might acquire

the habit of aiding his fellows; and the habit of performing benevolent actions certainly strengthens the feeling of sympathy, which gives the first impulse to benevolent actions. Habits, moreover, followed during many generations probably tend to be inherited.

In the same book, Darwin also tied morality in with what he referred to as "tribes."

It must not be forgotten that although a high standard of morality gives but a slight or no advantage to each individual man and his children over the other men of the same tribe, yet that an advancement in the standard of morality and an increase in the number of well-endowed men will certainly give an immense advantage to one tribe over another.

This is cause for no big comment because the causal processes are the same as for the rest of evolution.

There can be no doubt that a tribe including many members who, from possessing in a high degree the spirit of patriotism, fidelity, obedience, courage, and sympathy, were always ready to give aid to each other and to sacrifice themselves for the common good, would be victorious over most other tribes; and this would be natural selection.

Hence:

At all times throughout the world tribes have supplanted other tribes; and as morality is one element in their success, the standard of morality and the number of well-endowed men will thus everywhere tend to rise and increase.

There was no essential difference here from the thinking about social groups that we find in the *Origin*. Tribes for Darwin were akin to the nest of the ants or the hive of the bees. This point comes through in a letter that Darwin penned later in the decade to his son

George about an article that the philosopher Henry Sidgwick wrote in 1876 in an opening issue of the journal *Mind*:

Down Beckenham Kent

Ap. 27 th

My dear George

I send "Mind"—it seems an excellent periodical—Sidgwicks article has interested me much.—It is wonderfully clear & makes me feel what a muddle-headed man I am.—I do not agree on one point, however, with him. He speaks of moral men arising in a tribe, accidentally, i.e. by so-called spontaneous variation; but I have endeavoured to show that such men are created by love of glory, approbation &c &c.—However they appear the tribe as a tribe will be successful in the battle of life, like a hive of bees or nest of ants. We are off to London directly, but I am rather bad. Leonard comes home on May 10 th !! Plans changed.

Darwin was thinking of tribes, nests, and families as he had thought about the Hymenoptera in the *Origin*; in other words, as in some sense super-organisms, with the members as parts of the whole. But this came very naturally to him, embedded as he was in his own family—he was married to a first cousin and his older sister was married to a brother of his wife. With this proviso, however, Darwin never deviated from his belief that ultimately selection always occurred between individuals, and hence, adaptations must rebound to the benefit of individual, and only secondarily to groups, if at all.

Darwin also touched upon religion, although briefly. It is clear that by this stage of his life, like so many Victorians, he was rather inclined to think that traditional religion was rooted in superstition. When writing the *Origin*, the deism was still there, as he made clear in a celebrated letter written a few months later to Asa Gray: "I am inclined to look at everything as resulting from designed laws, with the details, whether good or bad, left to the working out of what we may call chance." Elaborating: "I can see no reason, why a man, or other animal, may not have been aboriginally produced by... laws; & that all these laws may have been expressly designed by an omniscient Creator, who foresaw every future event & consequence."

By the time of the *Descent*, probably thanks to the influence of Huxley who was trumpeting his "agnosticism," even that kind of belief had gone. A discreet Englishman, Darwin did not come out and say this bluntly, but he looked upon religion as something of a byproduct, brought about by incidental factors. For instance, he likened religious responses to nature to the excitement shown by one of his dogs when a parasol fluttered in the wind. It was not so much that Darwin was antireligious, but that he no longer found religion particularly relevant to his life, nor could he see much reason it had to be relevant to the lives of others.

Although Darwin was not as fanatical about progress as earlier evolutionists (and this was still true of people like Herbert Spencer), it is clear from the *Descent* that Darwin believed fully that human species had come out on top. Moreover, among humans, the Europeans had fared best of all. In later editions of the *Origin*, Darwin speculated that a form of progress could occur because better quality organisms were always beating out lesser quality ones:

> If we look at the differentiation and specialisation of the several organs of each being when adult (and this will include the advancement of the brain for intellectual purposes) as the best standard of highness of organisation, natural selection clearly leads towards highness; for all physiologists admit that the specialisation of organs, inasmuch as they perform in this state their functions better, is an advantage to each being; and hence the accumulation of variations tending towards specialisation is within the scope of natural selection.

Overall, this could accumulate until one got some kind of progress approaching absolute value. There was not much explicit discussion of any of this in the *Descent of Man*, but it was certainly presupposed. Rather more explicit was the notion that hard-working business people, like the Darwin-Wedgwood clan, had claim to being at the top of any ordering, combined with more than a hint of Puritan disapproval of those who were born to wealth and squandered it:

> In all civilised countries man accumulates property and bequeaths it to his children. So that the children in the same country do not by any means start fair in the race for success. But this is far from an unmixed evil; for without the accumulation of capital the arts could not progress; and it is chiefly through their power that the civilised races have extended, and are now everywhere extending, their range, so as to take the place of the lower races. Nor does the moderate accumulation of wealth interfere with the process of selection. When a poor man becomes rich, his children enter trades or professions in which there is struggle enough, so that the able in body and mind succeed best. The presence of a body of well-instructed men, who have not to labour for their daily bread, is important to a degree which cannot be over-estimated; as all high intellectual work is carried on by them, and on such work material progress of all kinds mainly depends, not to mention other and higher advantages. No doubt wealth when very great tends to convert men into useless drones, but their number is never large; and some degree of elimination here occurs, as we daily see rich men, who happen to be fools or profligate, squandering away all their wealth.

Interestingly, however, Darwin was not much inclined to think that modern Europeans triumphed over native races because of their superior fighting or intellectual abilities. Rather, Europeans had better natural immunities to diseases than indigenous people.

Hence, when the two groups mixed and interacted it was much more likely that natives would succumb to common diseases like measles.

It is clear also that Darwin thought sexual selection would play a role here. Thanks to the struggle for mates, better quality males would emerge. Also, more attractive females would prevail thanks to selection for beauty and related features. As he wrote:

> The strongest and most vigorous men,–those who could best defend and hunt for their families, and during later times the chiefs or head-men,–those who were provided with the best weapons and who possessed the most property, such as a larger number of dogs or other animals, would have succeeded in rearing a greater average number of offspring, than would the weaker, poorer and lower members of the same tribes. There can, also, be no doubt that such men would generally have been able to select the more attractive women.

This referred to sexual selection due to male combat or competition. There would also be place for sexual selection through female choice:

> [W]ith savages the women are not in quite so abject a state in relation to marriage as has often been supposed. They can tempt the men whom they prefer, and can sometimes reject those whom they dislike, either before or after marriage. Preference on the part of the women, steadily acting in any one direction, would ultimately affect the character of the tribe; for the women would generally choose not merely the handsomer men, according to their standard of taste, but those who were at the same time best able to defend and support them. Such well-endowed pairs would commonly rear a larger number of offspring than the less well endowed. The same result would obviously follow in a still more marked manner if there was selection on both sides; that is

if the more attractive, and at the same time more powerful men were to prefer, and were preferred by, the more attractive women. And these two forms of selection seem actually to have occurred, whether or not simultaneously, with mankind, especially during the earlier periods of our long history.

The "Hottentot Venus," Sarah Bartman, fascinated Europeans. In the Descent of Man, Darwin assures his readers that many natives find large bottoms very attractive and that in some tribes women are lined up so the most successful men can choose the females who protrude farthest "a tergo."

Do not put too much trust in this apparent balancing of the role of the sexes. Although Darwin was a great revolutionary, he was no rebel. This is shown very clearly by his assumptions about the superiority of Europeans over the natives, and even more so by his unquestioned belief that males were far more intelligent on average than females:

> The chief distinction in the intellectual powers of the two sexes is shewn by man attaining to a higher eminence, in whatever he takes up, than woman can attain—whether requiring deep thought, reason, or imagination, or merely the use of the senses and hands. If two lists were made of the most eminent men and women in poetry, painting, sculpture, music,—comprising composition and performance, history, science, and philosophy, with half a-dozen names under each subject, the two lists would not bear comparison.

In Darwin's view, females compensated by being creatures of emotion and sympathy. In other words, brains were for men and hearts for women!

In the next chapter, we will look at Darwin's hopes that the *Origin* would change the popular science of his day.

6. Popular Science

Charles Darwin entered the scene when evolution was a pseudo-science. Given his careful attention to the methodologies of his day, it had obviously been Darwin's hope that the *Origin* would elevate evolutionary studies to the level of a professional science, like physics and chemistry. He wanted natural selection to be a fruitful mechanism of inquiry. However, he failed in this aim. He convinced the world that evolution was a fact, but he did not succeed in persuading his fellow scientists that natural selection was an active and valuable tool of inquiry, giving us insights into the nature of organisms and their histories. It is true that there was some limited study of evolutionary morphology in the universities, but by and large, evolution was not a science for the professional scholar.

Evolution as popular science

To leave the story just like this would not do Darwin—or history—justice. We must turn now to the huge impact that the *Origin* and the *Descent* had on general culture. Evolution had not yet achieved the status of a professional science; it was, above all, the preeminent *popular science*—the science of the general domain. We see this most obviously in the new museums of natural history that were being built in Britain, on the continent, and particularly in the great cities of the United States of America. It was there that one went to see the wonderful panoramas of biological change—from primitive forms up through lesser animals until one reached the primates with humans at the peak. With the fabulous finds of fossil dinosaurs in the USA and Canada in the second half of the 19th century, museums became focal points of immense popular interest, playing the role of purveyors of popular science, which taught about the world and, at the same time, gave messages and understanding of moral, social, and religious issues.

After the enormous success of the Great Exhibition of 1851, the Crystal Palace was moved to a park in South London. In the grounds were placed models of dinosaurs, still there today. The brutes were shown as clumsy and massive, whereas now—as was shown in the movie Jurassic Park—there is the realization that many dinosaurs were agile and very active.

A conscious effort was made by the promoters of science like Thomas Henry Huxley to replace what they saw as their greatest rival, religion, especially the established Church of England. Consciously, natural history museums were modeled on Cathedrals, with the hope that instead of going to Communion on Sunday morning families would go to look at fossils and other fascinating and instructive objects on Sunday afternoons. This picture has the medieval Cathedral of Laon in France on top and the British Museum (Natural History) on the bottom.

Museums were for Sundays, the day of the family outing. What about the weekdays? This was before the advent of television, radio, and motion pictures. Universal literacy made enormous strides forward in the middle of the 19th century and the printed word—fiction and poetry—reigned supreme. Leading novelists like

Charles Dickens and poets like Alfred Tennyson were lionized, and they, in turn, reflected and molded public opinion. We have seen already how a beginning novelist like Thomas Hardy–a man who read Darwin with enthusiasm when young and who continued to regard the *Origin* as most influential on his thinking–picked up and used evolutionary themes. Through the last decades of the 19th century, this major role of the fact of evolution continued strong. In several of his novels and short stories, H. G. Wells, a student of Thomas Henry Huxley, also toyed with evolutionary themes, most notably in the *Time Machine*, where he supposed that human evolution had gone on to produce two new species, the beautiful but idle Eloi living above ground and the hardworking, but vile Morlocks dwelling in caves below ground and preying on those living above in the open. Likewise, evolution underlined much of the happenings in the classic vampire novel, *Dracula*, in which an evil fiend showed all of the features of our simian past. And similar themes played out in works like Arthur Conan Doyle's *The Lost World*, imagining an island of prehistoric beasts far away in South America. Incidentally, Conan Doyle's most famous creation, Sherlock Holmes, was apparently ignorant of the Copernican system but was well up on his Darwin!

Selection

I have written about the failure of natural selection as a scientifically convincing mechanism. Not so in the world of many creative writers, who saw it as a truly liberating idea. For instance, George Gissing's *New Grub Street*,–a story of struggling writers–explored the features needed for success or those that led to defeat, and how they played out together. This novel culminates with the loser dying and the winner marrying the loser's widow. As noted in this work, "though she had never opened one of Darwin's books, her knowledge of his main theories and illustrations was respectable." Most over-heated of all are the tales of the American novelist Jack

London, but one can see the raw power and how Darwin had changed our world. In his seminal novel, *The Call of the Wild*, London wrote:

> Buck possessed a quality that made for greatness—imagination. He fought by instinct, but he could fight by head as well. He rushed, as though attempting the old shoulder trick, but at the last instant swept low to the snow and in. His teeth closed on Spitz's left fore leg. There was a crunch of breaking bone, and the white dog faced him on three legs. Thrice he tried to knock him over, then repeated the trick and broke the right fore leg. Despite the pain and helplessness, Spitz struggled madly to keep up. He saw the silent circle, with gleaming eyes, lolling tongues, and silvery breaths drifting upward, closing in upon him as he had seen similar circles close in upon beaten antagonists in the past. Only this time he was the one who was beaten. There was no hope for him. Buck was inexorable. Mercy was a thing reserved for gentler climes.

Laugh in a condescending manner if you will, but the fact is that in its 100-year lifespan, this novel has never been out of print. At my last count, *Amazon.com* had over 30 different editions, and I am not separating hard- and soft-cover versions.

More subtle and perhaps more interesting was a novelist-poet like Hardy, who took away the message that the Darwinian mechanism was essentially unguided—the variations on which selection worked had no built-in teleology. In his novel *Tess of the D'Urbervilles*—a story with the high point in the penultimate paragraph where the heroine was hanged for murder, followed by the final paragraph where the hero went off with her sister and there was no felt need to remark that they would be unable to marry because such unions were banned by law—Hardy explored in unrelenting detail how fate offered no solace to the fragile human and how the meaningless of life could crush us all:

Upon the cornice of the tower a tall staff was fixed. Their eyes were riveted on it. A few minutes after the hour had struck something moved slowly up the staff, and extended itself upon the breeze. It was a black flag.

'Justice' was done, and the President of the Immortals, in Aeschylean phrase, had ended his sport with Tess. And the d'Urberville knights and dames slept on in their tombs unknowing. The two speechless gazers bent themselves down to the earth, as if in prayer, and remained thus a long time, absolutely motionless: the flag continued to wave silently. As soon as they had strength, they arose, joined hands again, and went on.

However, not everyone was quite this gloomy. And when it came to sexual selection, there was unbridled enthusiasm. Female protagonists in Gissing's *New Grub Street* knew the score. This is how one of them described a young journalist, Jasper Milvain:

He was so human, and a youth of all but monastic seclusion had prepared her to love the man who aimed with frank energy at the joys of life. A taint of pedantry would have repelled her. She did not ask for high intellect or great attainments; but vivacity, courage, determination to succeed, were delightful to her senses.

It was widely accepted that Darwin had spotted something important, and every human being could take consolation in the fact that love had taken the course nature intended. Constance Naden, a lively English poet of the 1880s, had tremendous fun in her *Evolutional Erotics*. Her protagonist—a young lover—was sure he was destined for success—after all, he was a successful and hard-working junior scientist. But, as Naden noted in the poem, his qualifications were not impressive enough:

But there comes an idealess lad,
With a strut, and a stare, and a smirk;

And I watch, scientific though sad,
The Law of Selection at work.
  Of Science he hasn't a trace,
He seeks not the How and the Why,
But he sings with an amateur's grace,
And he dances much better than I.
  And we know the more dandified males
By dance and by song win their wives –
'Tis a law that with *Avis* prevails,
And even in *Homo* survives.

In the end, the poor sap was left only with the reflection that science had predicted his fate all along:

Shall I rage as they whirl in the valse?
Shall I sneer as they carol and coo?
Ah no! for since Chloe is false,
I'm certain that Darwin is true!

Expectedly, there were those—like English poet May Kendall—who turned Darwin back on himself, arguing that, ultimately, his principles led to a sort of evolutionary feminism, as depicted in Kendall's 1880s poem, *Woman's Future*:

Complacent they tell us, hard hearts and derisive,
In vain is our ardour: in vain are our sighs:
Our intellects, bound by a limit decisive,
To the level of Homer's may never arise.
We heed not the falsehood, the base innuendo,
The laws of the universe, these are our friends,
Our talents shall rise in a mighty crescendo,
We trust Evolution to make us amends!

Interestingly, the poem refers to Darwin's fellow evolutionist, the previously mentioned Herbert Spencer:

Is this your vocation? My goal is another,

And empty and vain is the end you pursue.
In antimacassars the world you may smother;
But intellect marches o'er them and o'er you.
  On Fashion's vagaries your energies strewing,
Devoting your days to a rug or a screen,
Oh, rouse to a lifework – do something worth doing!
Invent a new planet, a flying-machine.
Mere charms superficial, mere feminine graces,
That fade or that flourish, no more you may prize;
But the knowledge of Newton will beam from your faces,
The soul of a Spencer will shine in your eyes.

Darwinism—and this means natural and sexual selection—was simply part of Victorian culture. And with people like Huxley and others (whom I shall mention in a moment) spreading the word in the New World, it was becoming part of American culture as well.

Religious reactions

By about 1870, most people accepted the fact of evolution. But many of the religious still found it very threatening. English poet Christina Georgina Rossetti started one of her sonnets by stressing the miraculous (i.e. religion-based) creation of the first humans:

Thou Who didst make and knowest whereof we are made,
Oh bear in mind our dust and nothingness...

And she then goes on to pick up the implications of the Creation:

Thou knowest,–remember Thou whereof we are made.
If making makes us Thine, then Thine we are;
And if redemption, we are twice Thine own:
If once Thou didst come down from heaven afar
To seek us and to find us, how not save?

Comfort us, save us, leave us not alone,
Thou Who didst die our death and fill our grave.

On a broader level, what is important to keep in mind is that by the 1860s, religion in Britain was in crisis-mode, and this phenomenon occurred irrespective of science. The effects of progressive German scholarship on biblical belief were proving ever more corrosive, and there was also an increasing number of home-grown critics. In 1860, a group of liberal churchmen published *Essays and Reviews*, challenging one comforting belief after another, and including a vigorous endorsement of Darwinism by the Reverend Baden Powell, professor at Oxford (and, incidentally, the father of the founder of the Scouting movement). John Colenso, Church of England's Bishop of Natal and author of popular mathematical textbooks, caused a huge row when he applied his numerical skills to the Old Testament and discovered that the claims and demands led to ludicrous figures. It is no wonder that the all-time best-seller of the late Victorian era was a novel titled *Robert Elsmere*, written in 1888 by Mrs. Humphrey Ward (Mary Augusta Ward). It is a story relating an Anglican clergyman's doubts about his church's doctrine:

'Do I *believe in God?* Surely, surely! "Though He slay me yet will I trust in Him!" *Do I believe in Christ?* Yes,–in the teacher, the martyr, the symbol to us Westerns of all things heavenly and abiding, the image and pledge of the invisible life of the spirit–with all my soul and all my mind!'

'*But in the Man-God*, the Word from Eternity,–in a wonder-working Christ, in a risen and ascended Jesus, in the living Intercessor and Mediator for the lives of His doomed brethren?'

He waited, conscious that it was the crisis of his history, and there rose in him, as though articulated one by one by an audible voice, words of irrevocable meaning.

'Every human soul in which the voice of God makes itself felt, enjoys, equally with Jesus of Nazareth, the divine sonship, and *"miracles do not happen!"*'

It was done.

After admitting his crisis of faith, Elsmere found himself doing social work in the East End of London. He succumbed to one of the mysterious ailments that afflicted many Victorian heroes—he mistook a serious (and ultimately fatal) malady for merely a bad case of "clergyman's throat." After Elsmere's death his widow—having covered her options by going to church in the morning—devoted her afternoons to continuing the work of her late husband, whose true saintly nature she recognized only on his deathbed.

It is little wonder that, by and large, religious people wanted to stay out of the Darwinian controversy. There were, however, some exceptions—foremost among them were the evangelicals of the American South (more about them later). Also, towards the end of the 19th century, the Catholic Church became increasingly opposed to the whole idea of evolution, but this was less on either theological or scientific grounds, and more a general opposition to modernism, as well as the political difficulties facing the Church in the newly unified Italy. But overall, despite the well-known stories of opposition, things were quieter than one might have expected. Reactions varied widely. Some people, like clergyman and evolutionist Charles Kingsley, were positive:

> I have gradually learnt to see that it is just as noble a conception of Deity, to believe that he created primal forms capable of self development into all forms needful pro tempore and pro loco, as to believe that He required a fresh act of intervention to supply the lacunas which He Himself had made. I question whether the former be not the loftier thought.

Others were inclined to go the route of Alfred Tennyson, trying to meld what they saw as an upwards evolutionary climb to humankind with their Christian belief in the special status of our own species—"made in the image of God."

Then there were those who accepted evolution but basically

declared it irrelevant to matters of faith. This was the view of John Henry Newman, a great theologian who began life as an Evangelical Protestant and became known as the "Prince of the Catholic Church." Perhaps not surprisingly, this view was shared by the great Jesuit poet Gerard Manley Hopkins. As his poem *That Nature is a Heraclitean Fire and of the comfort of the Resurrection* shows, initially it seemed as if the Darwinian message were a threat:

Delightfully the bright wind boisterous ropes, wrestles, beats earth bare
Of yestertempest's creases; in pool and rut peel parches
Squandering ooze to squeezed dough, crust, dust; stanches, starches
Squadroned masks and manmarks treadmire toil there
Footfretted in it. Million-fuelèd, nature's bonfire burns on.
But quench her bonniest, dearest to her, her clearest-selvèd spark
Man, how fast his firedint, his mark on mind, is gone!
Both are in an unfathomable, all is in an enormous dark
Drowned. O pity and indignation! Manshape, that shone
Sheer off, disseveral, a star, death blots black out; nor mark
Is any of him at all so stark
But vastness blurs and time beats level.

Fortunately, this was but part of the story. Read on:

Enough! the Resurrection,
A heart's-clarion! Away grief's gasping, joyless days, dejection.
Across my foundering deck shone
A beacon, an eternal beam. Flesh fade, and mortal trash
Fall to the residuary worm; world's wildfire, leave but ash:
In a flash, at a trumpet crash,
I am all at once what Christ is, since he was what I am, and
This Jack, joke, poor potsherd, patch, matchwood, immortal

diamond,
Is immortal diamond.

John Henry Newman (1801-1890). Like a lot of Christians, he basically thought that evolution had little or nothing to do with the essential elements of his religious beliefs. He was perfectly comfortable with the idea of Darwin receiving an honorary doctorate from his alma mater, Oxford University.

Evolution was not denied; it was just declared irrelevant. But this was certainly a minority view. For the majority, including for most religious people, the perception of the world had changed. Darwin and Spencer even managed to impact the field of philosophy.

American Pragmatism

Huxley always fancied himself a bit of a philosopher. He wrote a book about David Hume, "with helps to the study of Berkeley." A couple of years before his death, Huxley gave a lecture on evolution and ethics that was not particularly well received at the time, but had later gained recognition as a powerful tract about the implications of evolution for moral behavior, and how simplistic inferences from the one to the other were false to the point of being dangerous. Interestingly, when he was not writing as a scientist, Huxley took it for granted that an understanding of natural selection was crucial to the topic. In *Evolution and Ethics*, he wrote:

> All plants and animals exhibit the tendency to vary, the causes of which have yet to be ascertained; it is the tendency of the conditions of life, at any given time, while favouring the existence of the variations best adapted to them, to oppose that of the rest and thus to exercise selection; and all living things tend to multiply without limit, while the means of support are limited; the obvious cause of which is the production of offspring more numerous than their progenitors, but with equal expectation of life in the actuarial sense. Without the first tendency there could be no evolution. Without the second, there would be no good reason why one variation should disappear and another take its place; that is to say, there would be no selection. Without the third, the struggle for existence, the agent of the selective process in the state of nature, would vanish.

Darwin himself could not have said it better. Huxley continued:

> So far as it tends to make any human society more efficient in the struggle for existence with the state of nature, or with other societies, it works in harmonious contrast with the cosmic process. But it is none the less true that, since law and morals are restraints upon the struggle for existence between men in society, the ethical process is in opposition to the principle of the cosmic process, and tends to the suppression of the qualities best fitted for success in that struggle.

Writing at about the same time as Gissing, both agreed on the concept of the struggle. The only difference was that Gissing was happy with the consequences, while Huxley was less certain.

Whether Huxley was right in thinking that morality demanded a fight against our nature is a matter to which we shall return. For now, crossing the Atlantic, we find that in the philosophical circles of the New World Darwin's theories had a huge and much more positive influence. The ideas outlined in The *Descent of Man*, especially some of the side comments that Darwin made about language and culture, were appreciated and developed. It is worth quoting in full what Darwin had to say about language:

> The formation of different languages and of distinct species, and the proofs that both have been developed through a gradual process, are curiously the same. But we can trace the origin of many words further back than in the case of species, for we can perceive that they have arisen from the imitation of various sounds, as in alliterative poetry. We find in distinct languages striking homologies due to community of descent, and analogies due to a similar process of formation. The manner in which certain letters or sounds change when others change is very like correlated growth. We have in both cases the reduplication of parts, the effects of long-continued use, and so forth. The frequent presence

of rudiments, both in languages and in species, is still more remarkable. The letter m in the word am, means I; so that in the expression I am, a superfluous and useless rudiment has been retained. In the spelling also of words, letters often remain as the rudiments of ancient forms of pronunciation. Languages, like organic beings, can be classed in groups under groups; and they can be classed either naturally according to descent, or artificially by other characters. Dominant languages and dialects spread widely and lead to the gradual extinction of other tongues. A language, like a species, when once extinct, never, as Sir C. Lyell remarks, reappears.

Darwin continued:

The same language never has two birth-places. Distinct languages may be crossed or blended together. We see variability in every tongue, and new words are continually cropping up; but as there is a limit to the powers of the memory, single words, like whole languages, gradually become extinct. As Max Müller has well remarked:–"A struggle for life is constantly going on amongst the words and grammatical forms in each language. The better, the shorter, the easier forms are constantly gaining the upper hand, and they owe their success to their own inherent virtue." To these more important causes of the survival of certain words, mere novelty may, I think, be added; for there is in the mind of man a strong love for slight changes in all things. The survival or preservation of certain favoured words in the struggle for existence is natural selection.

Notice how this is a modification–or perhaps extension–of natural selection. We do not have the literal success of one organism over another, but rather of one word over another. Or, perhaps more precisely, since obviously words as such do not triumph in their use by one speaker over another, or the same speaker at different times.

One who picked up on this was the early American Pragmatist, Chauncey Wright—a fanatical Darwinian much appreciated by the master himself, who had reprinted at his own expense one of Wright's reviews of a book very critical of evolution by natural selection. Wright wrote:

> In the development of language, its separations into the varieties of dialects, the divergences of these into species, or distinct languages, and the affinities of them as grouped by the glossologist into genera of languages, present precise parallels to the developments and relations in the organic world which the theory of natural selection supposes.

Notice that this is not just evolution, but "the theory of natural selection."

Along the same lines, although now extending to talk of influential individuals in the society, there was the better-known Pragmatist, brother of the novelist Henry James, William James. In one of his philosophy essays, he wrote:

> The causes of production of great men lie in a sphere wholly inaccessible to the social philosopher. He must simply accept geniuses as data, just as Darwin accepts his spontaneous variations. For him, as for Darwin, the only problem is, these date being given, how does the environment affect them, and how do they affect the environment? Now, I affirm that the relation of the visible environment to the great man is in the main exactly what it is to the "variation" in the Darwinian philosophy. It chiefly adopts or rejects, preserves or destroys, in short selects him. And whenever it adopts and preserves the great man, it becomes modified by his influence in an entirely original and peculiar way. He acts as a ferment, and changes its constitution, just as the advent of a new zoölogical species changes the faunal and floral equilibrium of the region in which it appears.

He went on to say:

> The mutations of societies, then, from generation to generation, are in the main due directly or indirectly to the acts or the examples of individuals whose genius was so adapted to the receptivities of the moment, or whose accidental position of authority was so critical that they became ferments, initiators of movements, setters of precedent or fashion, centers of corruption, or destroyers of other persons, whose gifts, had they had free play, would have led society in another direction.

More broadly, James saw the Darwinian process integrated into the very fabric of thinking, for "the new conceptions, emotions, and active tendencies which evolve are originally produced in the shape of random images, fancies, accidental out-births of spontaneous variation in the functional activity of the excessively instable human brain, which the outer environment simply confirms or refutes, adopts or rejects, preserves or destroys,–selects, in short, just as it selects morphological and social variations dues to molecular accidents of an analogous sort." It is all there. In nature, there is a struggle for existence, with consequent evolution in the direction of adaptive excellence. In culture, there is a struggle for existence between ideas, with consequent evolution in the direction of adaptive excellence in the world of knowledge."

The American Pragmatist, William James (1842–1910). The early novels of his brother, Henry James, especially The Portrait of a Lady (1881), show strong Darwinian influences, especially in the use of sexual selection as a structuring theme.

One cannot overemphasize the importance of this kind of thinking and its subsequent influence on American thought and life, especially through the field of education and the use that was made of Pragmatism by philosopher John Dewey, a major voice for progressive education and social reform. Still, for much of the 20th century, Darwin-infused thinking was not much appreciated in the field of academic philosophy in both Britain and America. There were reasons for this, primarily that one of the greatest influences—the English-born philosopher Bertrand Russell—was educated at a time when the star of Herbert Spencer shone brightly, and he, therefore, thought of evolution primarily in Spencerian terms. There was perhaps a tinge of anti-Americanism in Russell's thinking and (somewhat more to his credit) a fear that Pragmatism might have unfortunate social and political consequences. As he wrote:

> Pragmatism, in some of its forms, is a power-philosophy. For pragmatism, a belief is 'true' if its consequences are pleasant. Now human beings can make the consequences of a belief pleasant or unpleasant. Belief in the moral superiority of a dictator has pleasanter consequences than disbelief, if you live under his government. Wherever there is effective persecution, the official creed is 'true' in the pragmatist sense. The pragmatist philosophy, therefore, gives to those in power a metaphysical omnipotence which a more pedestrian philosophy would deny to them.

Be this as it may, Pragmatism was important and, as we will see, since the 1960s Darwinism has been making a comeback, even in Anglophone philosophical circles. For now, we can bring to an end our brief survey of the impact of Darwinism—as pertaining to natural and sexual selection—on general culture in Britain and America. When you look at the broader context, talk of a "non-Darwinian revolution" is simply ludicrous.

In the next chapter, we will explore Darwinian thought in the context "professional" science.

7. Professional Science

After the *Origin*, probably the most important event in the history of evolutionary theory was the work on the principles of heredity carried out in the 1860s by the Moravian monk, Gregor Mendel. (Or, perhaps more pertinently, the rediscovery of his work at the beginning of the 20th century.) People often regret that Darwin and Mendel were working independently. If only they had gotten together and collaborated, then the course of evolution might have been advanced significantly, much earlier than it was. In fact, Mendel was working on rather technical questions about plant breeding. It is highly improbable that had Darwin read his work, he would have grasped its full significance. Conversely, Mendel did, in fact, read the *Origin of Species* but he never once thought that what he was doing contributed to the story. Instead, from Mendel's marginalia, we can infer that the big question that the *Origin* posed to him focused on whether this theory was acceptable to a Catholic priest!

GREGOR MENDEL.
Abbot of Brünn
Born 1822. Died 1884.

From a photograph kindly supplied by the Very Rev. Dr Janetschek, the present Abbot.

Gregor Mendel (1822-1884). In the last decade of his life, Mendel gave up science and, elected abbot of his monastery, became an administrator, not realizing that in the twentieth century he would become one of the most famous scientists of all time. Statistical studies have shown that Mendel's reported results were too good to be true, giving rise to endless speculation about whether Mendel consciously fudged his results or was simply naïve about the experimental method. The most satisfying solution is to blame someone else, the gardening assistants!

Becoming a professional science

Once rediscovered, Mendel's ideas were developed quickly and fused with a growing understanding of the physical nature of the organic cell. By the middle of the second decade of the 20th century, evolutionary biologist Thomas Hunt Morgan and his students at Columbia University in New York City had developed the so-called "classical theory of the gene." This theory saw the unit of heredity, the gene, as a particle on one of those long, string-like entities—chromosomes—in the center of the cell, the nucleus. Chromosomes come in pairs, so genes are paired, and by the time of reproduction one of each gene pair gets passed on through the sex cells to the next generation. The important thing is that the genes remain unchanged from generation to generation, occasionally changing when they spontaneously "mutate" from one form to another. As Darwin supposed, mutation was random in the sense that it did not occur according to need, but it was not random in the sense of being uncaused. Today much more is known about the physical causes of mutation.

Perhaps expectedly, when Mendelian genetics was first rediscovered, its supporters thought that it offered a rival theory to a Darwinian picture of evolution through natural selection. For a while, there was a bitter controversy between the Darwinian "biometricians" and the Mendelian "geneticists." However, by the second decade of the 20th-century, biologists were starting to see that Darwinian selection and Mendelian genetics were not contradictory but complementary parts of the whole picture. Because selection works only on groups and not on single individuals, it was necessary to generalize Mendelian genetics to cover populations. This was done by two researchers after whom the key premise, the Hardy-Weinberg law, is named.

In Newtonian mechanics, his first law (that bodies remain at rest or in uniform motion unless acted upon by a force) acted as an equilibrium law, against which one could introduce intervening or distorting forces. In "population genetics," the Hardy-Weinberg law had the same function. This law essentially stated that in large populations with no impinging forces—such as selection, mutation, immigration or emigration—the gene ratios would stay constant. In other words, it was the background equilibrium against which one could now introduce distorting forces like mutation and selection.

Around 1930, several mathematically gifted biologists developed this theory, which is the basis of evolutionary thinking even to this day. In England, particularly important were Ronald A. Fisher and J. B. S. Haldane; in America, Sewall Wright's work was significant. Although their theories were formally equivalent, the English and the Americans (Fisher and Wright particularly) had very different visions of the evolutionary process. For Fisher, it was always Darwin's mechanism first and foremost, as he saw populations being molded and shaped by natural selection occurring on new variations, mutations. For Wright, things were rather more complex. Although he gave selection an important role in his "shifting balance theory" of evolution, random forces or effects were highly significant. Wright pointed out that, in small populations, the vagaries of breeding might be expected to overcome weak forces of selection. Hence, one might get ratios of genes "drifting" from one level to another. Wright believed that this was very important in the evolutionary process and consequently he was much more inclined to think that many features were adaptively neutral (whereas Fisher, with his selectionism, saw adaptation everywhere). We have here echoes of the differences that were expressed at the time of the *Origin*, with Darwin ultra-keen on adaptation and Huxley somewhat indifferent.

With the theory spelled out, the empiricists moved in. In England, particularly important was the Oxford biologist E. B. Ford. He was the founder of the school of evolutionists he labeled "ecological genetics." Ford and his collaborators worked extensively on organisms that reproduce rapidly, including butterflies, moths and small invertebrates like snails. Particularly noteworthy were some studies done in the 1950s by A. J. Cain and Philip Sheppard on the ways in which snail-shell colors and markings provide adaptive camouflage against predators, mainly thrushes. In the United States, the most important figure was the Russian-born geneticist Theodosius Dobzhansky. He was the author of *Genetics and the Origin of Species* (1937), a work in which he showed how Wright's shifting balance theory could be applied to many problems, particularly variations in Drosophila (fruit flies). Dobzhansky was also important for encouraging researchers in other fields to turn to evolutionary problems. Among them were the German-born systematist Ernst Mayr, author of *Systematics and the Origin of Species* (1942); the paleontologist George Gaylord Simpson, author of *Tempo and Mode in Evolution* (1944); and the botanist G. Ledyard Stebbins, author of *Variation and Evolution in Plants* (1950). Thanks to the work of these people, their collaborators and associates, and above all their students, by the 100th anniversary of the *Origin of Species* in 1959, Darwin's work had finally matured into a fully professional science. In England, it was known as "neo-Darwinism" and in America, paying tribute to Mendel as well as Darwin, as the "Synthetic theory of evolution."

The last half-century has seen a huge amount of work, both theoretical and empirical, tackling evolutionary problems from a Darwinian perspective. To give a flavor of what has been produced, it will be convenient to follow the pattern of the argument in the *Origin*. In that way, we will get an idea not only of what has been done but also how things have advanced since Darwin himself. Generally, the Darwinian belief in the ubiquity of adaptation has prevailed, although, as we will see, how this works in practice might be quite complex.

Artificial and natural selection

Let's start with artificial selection. There are now many case studies showing how continued, systematic selection by human beings can have huge effects on the genetically based nature of animals and plants. One justly famous example is a very long-term study (it started back in 1896) done at the University of Illinois on the oil content of corn (what Europeans call maize). At the beginning of the study, the oil content was in the range of 4% to 6%. By the end, in the 1970s, thanks to continued selection, the oil content had increased threefold to around 16%. This is change in itself. However, one objection that Darwin's contemporaries (notably Thomas Henry Huxley) often made was that artificial selection seemed never to lead to new species, meaning separate groups of organisms unable to interbreed. Today we have such cases. One experiment started with yellow and white varieties of corn. Selecting intensely for individuals that mated with others of the same color, in a very few generations, researchers produced two groups with very little cross-fertilization. It turned out that there was a good reason for this: the white variety flowered at an earlier time than the yellow variety, and hence pollination of the two varieties was kept separate.

Moving on to the key part of the *Origin* where natural selection was introduced, what evidence do we have today of this mechanism in action? Darwin himself thought that we would never have any direct observations of natural selection changing organisms. However, although I am not sure that Darwin picked up on the significance, late in his life one of his correspondents drew his attention to what today is probably the most famous example of evolution in action, the so-called "industrial melanism" (the development of the dark-colored pigment). By the middle of the 19th century in England, it was becoming clear that some species of butterfly had dark, melanic forms. In a letter he wrote to Darwin in 1878, entomologist A.B. Farn hypothesized that the reason for this pigmentation was industrial pollution. Butterflies rested on the trunks of trees and Farn pointed out that smoke and smog in the air made the bark increasingly darker and darker. Hence, given that the chief predators of butterflies were birds that hunted by sight, there was strong adaptive pressure towards darker forms, which would be easier to camouflage."

My dear Sir,

The belief that I am about to relate something which may be of interest to you, must be my excuse for troubling you with a letter.

Perhaps among the whole of the British Lepidoptera, no species varies more, according to the locality in which it is found, than does that Geometer, Gnophos obscurata. They are almost black on the New Forest peat; grey on limestone; almost white on the chalk near Lewes; and brown on clay, and on the red soil of Herefordshire.

Do these variations point to the "survival of the fittest"? I think so. It was, therefore, with some surprise that I took specimens as dark as any of those in the New Forest on a chalk slope; and I have pondered for a solution. Can this be it?

It is a curious fact, in connexion with these dark specimens, that for the last quarter of a century the chalk slope, on which they occur, has been swept by volumes of black smoke from some lime-kilns situated at the bottom: the herbage, although growing luxuriantly, is blackened by it.

I am told, too, that the very light specimens are now much less common at Lewes than formerly, and that, for some few years, lime-kilns have been in use there.

These are the facts I desire to bring to your notice.

I am, Dear Sir, Yours very faithfully,

A. B. Farn

Whether or not Darwin himself appreciated this point outlined by Mr. Farn—whose other claim to fame apparently was that of having killed 30 birds in 30 shots on the estate of Lord Walsingham, thus establishing a record "which has probably never been equaled"—by the end of the 19th-century melanism was a well-recognized phenomenon among students of butterflies and moths, and researchers realized that natural selection was at work. However, it was not until the middle of the 20th century that one of Ford's ecological geneticists, H. B. D. Kettlewell, working in areas around Oxford, finally showed definitively that the melanic forms of moths and butterflies were indeed sustained by selection for camouflage. Presciently, Kettlewell suggested that were pollution ever to be controlled, melanic forms would decline, and normal forms would regain their ascendancy. Since the 1950s, there has been in Britain a major overall drive to reduce air pollution. Consequently, trees today are far less blackened than they were 50 years ago. And as predicted, we find that the lighter forms of butterflies predominate, and melanic forms are significantly lower. This is a good example of natural selection observed in action.

Industrial melanism. The normal form stands out on a sooty background whereas the melanic form is camouflaged.

We need not dwell here at any length on the discoveries about heredity. We have seen already in this chapter that the field has been transformed since Darwin's days. Of course, genetics itself has not stood still. The major event after the rediscovery of Mendelian genetics was obviously the deciphering of the structure of the DNA molecule in 1953, by the American James Watson and the Englishman Francis Crick. The double helix led to a huge amount of work uncovering the basic secrets of heredity at the molecular level. Repeating an earlier pattern, at first, it was thought that the new field of genetics was a rival to Darwinian selection; but then, repeating an earlier pattern, it was seen how in major respects molecular biology was a handmaiden to the evolutionist. Most notably, in the 1960s, the geneticist Richard Lewontin and his associates used their knowledge of molecular biology, combined with new experimental techniques, to peer in much greater detail into the nature of variation in wild animals and plants. It will be remembered how important it was for Darwin's theory to have such variation. In its absence, natural selection is ineffectual. Using "gel electrophoresis," Lewontin and others showed just how much variation there was, leading to a level of understanding quite beyond anything that Darwin offered in the *Origin of Species*.

Consilience

What of the consilience of inductions? We have seen how this was a crucial part of the argumentation of the *Origin*, as Darwin strove to show that natural selection is a true cause. Simply put, the consilience as such exists unchanged in today's evolutionary studies. But it has been transformed completely by new findings and theories that have enriched our understanding of the different areas of the life sciences. Following Darwin, let us go briefly through social behavior, paleontology, biogeographical distributions, systematics, morphology, and embryology.

The study of the evolution of social behavior has seen explosive growth in the past half-century. "Sociobiology," as the field is now called, has many exciting discoveries to report. Thanks to the work of leading exponents—particularly William Hamilton in England and

Edward O. Wilson in America—we have a detailed and sophisticated grasp of how natural selection has shaped and molded the behaviors of organisms in groups. Particularly important was Hamilton's insight that organisms need not reproduce directly themselves. It is enough that close relatives (that is to say, organisms sharing the same genes) reproduce, so one does it by proxy, as it were. "Kin selection" has proven to be a very powerful tool for investigation. Sociobiologists have been able to analyze the relationships existing within groups of ants, bees, and wasps (Hymenoptera). They point to the fact that sterile workers share the same genes as their fertile nest mates and hence, inasmuch as they help these nest mates to reproduce, they are themselves reproducing, in the sense of passing on copies of the genes. In other words, today we can go a step beyond Darwin and show that nests need not be considered simply as united individuals. There can be different reproductive strategies even within the nest. However, what is still emphasized is Darwin's prime insight that ultimately selection works for the benefit of the individual and not the group. Not for nothing did the English biologist and popular science writer Richard Dawkins call his runaway bestseller *The Selfish Gene*. Of course, genes can be nothing of the kind, but the underlying truth is that all goes back to the individual, whether it be the organism or, in today's biological world, the gene.

Richard Dawkins (b. 1941). Dawkins today is as well known for his best-selling book on atheism, *The God Delusion*, giving rise to speculations about the extent to which a belief in Darwinism points one towards non-belief. There is obviously no necessary connection and some well-known Darwinians like Ronald Fisher and Theodosius Dobzhansky have been Christians, but perhaps there is an inclination.

One of Darwin's biggest problems regarding the fossil record was that it seemed to start abruptly in the Cambrian period. Darwin did not have absolute dates, but we know now that this occurred more than half a billion years ago. Adding to Darwin's worries, the earliest known organisms were extremely sophisticated invertebrates like trilobites. Where, then, were the simple Precambrian organisms that Darwin's theory presupposed? He spent much effort offering ad hoc hypotheses to explain the absence. Today, however, it is not necessary to invent such hypotheses because we have full and detailed knowledge of the fossil record going back nearly four billion years. Moreover, as expected, the very earliest organisms are very simple and then, coming up to the Cambrian era, they get more complex. I will return to the fossil record in the next chapter when talking about human origins.

The coming of continental drift, fueled by the mechanism of plate tectonics, had obviously transformed our understanding of the geographical distributions of organisms. We can today readily explain why we often find fossils representing the same species in very different parts of the world—for instance, in Africa, India, and Antarctica. It is simply because at some point in the past, these different landmasses were all joined and their inhabitants could roam freely across. The lands started to drift apart, and vast tracts of oceans separated the fossil remains of the earlier inhabitants.

At the same time, thanks to more sophisticated understandings about how organisms can travel from one area to another, today's evolutionists can throw considerable light on the relationships among the living organisms on different landmasses. For instance, there has been much successful effort devoted to the relationships between the inhabitants of North America and those of South America. It is shown how there was an interchange when the lands were joined, and how newcomers succeeded with greater or lesser success when they traveled into new ecological surroundings. The overall theory is still very Darwinian, but in all details, it has been completely transformed.

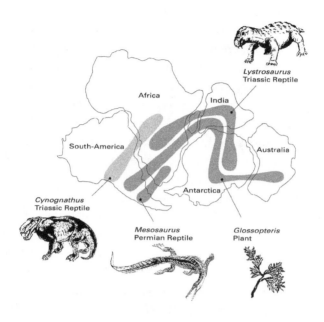

The distributions of some animals and plants as revealed by the fossil record and as explained by continental drift. The Triassic reptile Lystrosaurus is particularly striking. It was very sluggish and yet is to be found in Africa, in Indian, and in Antarctica.

Systematics underwent a major revolution of its own about 30 years ago. Thanks to new techniques, brought about in large part by the introduction of computers able to digest huge amounts of information, new ways of classifying organisms was devised. "Cladism" is a far more sophisticated way of working out genealogical relationships than anything that existed previously. It is true that some of the early enthusiasts for cladism were not Darwinians. They were not much interested in adaptation–after all, by the time the taxonomist gets to work, the specimens are usually dead and hence not using their body parts–and so tended to downplay the need for selection. But, with the passage of time, it has become more and more apparent that the classifications of today represent not just evolutionary relationships, but evolutionary relationships that were brought about by natural selection.

Some of the most exciting discoveries of all have occurred in morphology, considered in a broad sense. Thanks to molecular biology, we can now compare organisms right down to the most basic levels, far below the physical features known to Darwin and his contemporaries. Truly outstanding has been the way in which molecular biologists have been able to show that there are homologies in the DNA molecule between organisms very far apart, notably between humans and Drosophila (fruit flies). This does not disprove Darwinism. What it shows is that nature does not build each organism from scratch, as it were. Rather, organisms are built on modular principles, like Lego toys. We start with a set of different parts: building things one way we get fruit flies and building things another way we get humans. It is entirely analogous to Lego: building things one way we get the White House, and building things another way we get the Statue of Liberty. The important point is that it is selection that guides the process.

Finally, we come to embryology, or as it is known today "evolutionary development" (evo-devo). Again, there are echoes of the Huxley stand on adaptation. We find enthusiasts who suggest that selection is unimportant, merely acting as a garbage collector of failed new forms. Truly, this is not the case. What today's developmental biologists can show is that often change does not involve new genes making new characteristics. Rather, change comes about through adjusting rates of growth. By stretching an organism or increasing the number of segments, you can often make something very new indeed, without the need to find whole new body parts. But how it is determined which organisms survive and reproduce, and which do not, is, of course, a Darwinian matter. Selection monitors organisms in every generation. It never takes a break. In other words, as so often is the case, the new theories and Darwinian selection are complements rather than rivals.

Conclusion

The great Greek philosopher Heraclitus said "you cannot step into the same river twice," meaning that everything changes. The equally great Greek philosopher Parmenides said "nothing changes." The fate of Darwinian theory shows that both philosophers were right! Everything has changed since the days of the *Origin of Species*. Nothing has changed since the days of the *Origin of Species*. If Charles Darwin came back to earth today, he would be delighted.

In the next chapter, we will examine what today's Darwinians say about human evolution.

8. Humankind

C harles Darwin's theory of evolution through natural selection was always more than just a scientific theory. Early on, people recognized that it had significant implications throughout culture. In this concluding chapter, let us go back to this topic. As a start, what do we know now about our own origins?

Human evolution

Darwin knew little or nothing of the actual course of human evolution; he was never that interested in the actual course of change—of what people like Haeckel called "phylogeny." Neanderthals had been discovered, although general opinion—for instance, that of Huxley in *Man's Place in Nature*—was that they were, at best, merely a sub-species of humans. More than one person drew attention to the West-Coast Irish as possible exemplifications. It was not until almost the end of the 19th century that the first genuine "missing link"—Java Man—was discovered by the Dutch doctor Eugène Dubois. He put it in a different genus, *Pithecanthropus erectus*, but now, even though it was assigned to a different species, it is placed within our genus—Homo erectus. Dubois had no way of dating his finds but today we believe that Java Man was under a million years old. It walked upright, but its brain capacity was about 900 cubic centimeters (cc). By comparison, our brains measure about 1200 cc and sometimes more; chimpanzees' brains are about 400 cc. (No scientist believes that chimpanzees are our ancestors. But when our line—hominins—broke away from the other apes, our brain size was about that size).

As soon as the Origin was published, the Irish were portrayed as ape-like with lots of jokes about Mr. G. O'Rilla. This particular cartoon had the heading "King of A-Shantee," balancing prejudice against the Irish with prejudice against Africans through the pun on "shanty" (meaning a run-down house) and the Ashanti (an African tribe from Ghana).

In the second decade of the 20th century, one of the greatest hoaxes in the history of science was perpetrated in England. The discovery of Piltdown Man was a wonderful find, for apart from being British—Darwin would certainly have approved of that—it showed an exact transition with a human-like brain and an apelike jaw. Sadly, 30 years later it was revealed that the brain was indeed human, but the jaw was a stained orangutan bone. (One of the bones had been carved into the exact shape of a cricket bat!) Even now we are not sure about the identity of the trickster, although the discovery of some suggestive materials in a long-abandoned trunk made it clear that Martin Hinton, one of the curators at the British Museum, played a role in this affair. The sordid episode inspired the British writer Angus Wilson to produce a wonderful novel, *Anglo-Saxon Attitudes*. It is a marvelous psychological study of how someone sets out to play a mischievous trick on a pompous colleague and then finds himself plunged farther and farther into fraud and deceit as everyone takes his plot seriously.

Although Darwin believed all humans had African forefathers, most people did not want to find out that their ancestors were savages, to use the common term. However, this proved to be the case. First, there was Taung Baby, an australopithecine–a different genus from humans–discovered by Raymond Dart in South Africa in the 1920s. It did have a chimpanzee-size brain, and it was suggestive of the way the brain would have been attached to the body that it walked upright. A decade later in East Africa, archeologist Louis Leakey and his wife Mary worked to find fossil evidence of the human past. In mid-century, Leakey discovered the skull of a Miocene hominoid, an ape-like creature believed to have been a common ancestor of humans and other primate species. In 1960, Leakey and his team found evidence of another species, *Homo habilis*, believed to be a direct human ancestor. But the main prize surely goes to the American paleoanthropologist, Don Johanson, and his associates who, working in Ethiopia in 1974, discovered "Lucy," a female *Australopithecus afarensis*. Over three feet tall, she too had a chimpanzee-size brain, but as her full skeleton showed, she was fully bipedal though better at climbing trees than modern humans. A bit over three million years old, she provided the definitive answer to the question that plagued Darwin and his contemporaries–did we think first, or did we walk first. As it turned out, upright legs came first, and brains second.

Fossil discoveries continued to be made in the 21st century. Most exciting was the "hobbit," *Homo floresiensis*, a tiny being discovered at the beginning of the 2000s on an island in Indonesia. While it does not call for a radical rethinking of human evolution, there is controversy over whether it is a side branch that never grew or a group that found itself on an island and shrank—a phenomenon often recorded in island species. The presence of these fossils is important, of course, but even more significant in the recent history of paleoanthropology has been the discovery of the molecules and techniques for establishing not only the dates, but also relative points of kinship. We know, for instance, that humans are more closely related to chimpanzees than chimpanzees are to gorillas. We also know that the time of the divide was much shorter than we initially thought, although there is an on-going discussion about whether the accepted time span of five to six million years should be extended. What we also know—and this would have shocked the Victorians—is that our ancestors sometimes had relations with the Neanderthals, but only Europeans show this evidence of sub-specific dalliance. Apparently human beings left Africa in waves and those who stayed at home remained genetically pure. If we are talking about cavemen, then we are talking about white people and not about black people. (Incidentally, that most distinctive of dividers, human skin color, only occurred about 15,000 years ago.)

General culture

So much for the science. You might think, from a broad cultural perspective, that Darwin's time has passed. Apart from anything else, we saw in the last chapter that evolutionary theory became professionalized, with natural selection as the central mechanism. The days of popular science were numbered and gone. When evolutionary theory started to take its full place within the scientific realm, the social and other implications that made Darwinism so fascinating and important to the general public had weakened; however, this phenomenon had by no means precluded the continuation of a more popular dimension, even from the professional scientists themselves: people still worried about our place in nature. There has been an on-going concern about the struggle and the implications for humankind. Even the Irish poet W.B. Yeats picked up on the cruelty of nature and the struggle for existence. In his 1938 poem, *The Man and the Echo*, he wrote:

> O Rocky Voice,
> Shall we in that great night rejoice?
> What do we know but that we face
> One another in this place?
> But hush, for I have lost the theme,
> Its joy or night seem but a dream;
> Up there some hawk or owl has struck,
> Dropping out of sky or rock,
> A stricken rabbit is crying out,
> And its cry distracts my thought.

Sexual selection was not forgotten either, as is shown in this rather bittersweet sonnet, *I Shall Forget You Presently*, by Edna St. Vincent Millay:

> I shall forget you presently, my dear,
> So make the most of this, your little day,
> Your little month, your little half a year,
> Ere I forget, or die, or move away,
> And we are done forever; by and by
> I shall forget you, as I said, but now,
> If you entreat me with your loveliest lie
> I will protest you with my favorite vow.
> I would indeed that love were longer-lived,
> And oaths were not so brittle as they are,
> But so it is, and nature has contrived
> To struggle on without a break thus far,—

Whether or not we find what we are seeking
Is idle, biologically speaking.

One thing that made a full assessment of the significance of Darwinian ideas in the 20th century difficult was the existence of rival ideologies competing for attention. Sigmund Freud and Karl Marx, in particular, spring to mind. Sometimes different systems could co-exist harmoniously—Freud believed his thinking was rooted in evolutionary biology, although it tended to be more Lamarckian than Darwinian; at his funeral, Friedrich Engels famously said, "Just as Darwin discovered the law of development of organic nature, so Marx discovered the law of development of human history." Yet, at times there were conflicts and rivalry, especially in newer ideologies, pushing out Darwinism. For instance, Robert Louis Stevenson's novella, *Dr. Jekyll and Mr. Hyde,* has (along with a good dose of Calvinist thought about original sin) strong Darwinian undercurrents. As this passage shows, Mr. Hyde had simian traits:

Hence the ape-like tricks that he would play me, scrawling in my own hand blasphemies on the pages of my books, burning the letters and destroying the portrait of my father; and indeed, had it not been for his fear of death, he would long ago have ruined himself in order to involve me in the ruin.

By the time of the 1931 movie, Dr. Jekyll (played by Frederick March) had acquired a girlfriend not mentioned in the novella—in Stevenson's tale there are very strong hints that Dr. Jekyll was wracked by homosexual inclinations that could only be actualized through Mr. Hyde—and she had a father who didn't want her to rush into marriage with Jekyll, who already had naughty thoughts about a music-hall singer—also not mentioned in the novella—who was murdered by Mr. Hyde. The movie was made before the decency code kicked in and, although later six minutes were deleted to make it publicly palatable, the DVD version is now restored to its full

Freudian glory. This tale is a good example of repressed sexuality, of the unconscious having its wicked way, and of Oedipal urges so blatantly wanting to satisfy incestuous drives while cutting off the penises of younger rivals.

Nevertheless, without being triumphant, one senses that, to a large extent, Freud and Marx have had their day. More significantly, Darwin was never vanquished. In the 1930s, for instance, novelists like John Steinbeck explored Darwinian themes in the context of the Great Depression. *Grapes of Wrath* is hugely indebted to thoughts of possible change and of the ways in which biology can promote connections between warring groups. Then, in the 1950s, the Catholic novelist Graham Greene honed in on the evolutionary ideas of the French Jesuit priest, Teilhard de Chardin, who, in an almost Tennysonian fashion, saw the history of life as one long progression leading to humankind. At the same time, the future Nobel Prize winner William Golding meditated in his novel, *The Inheritors*, on the demise of the Neanderthals at the hands of our ancestors. And more recently, there has been an emergence of a minor industry in what is known as neo-Victorian novels, pastiches on the real things. I am not sure how Darwinian some of these works truly are—my favorite is *Fingersmith* by Sarah Waters, a horror-thriller spiced with a dash of lesbian sex. Judging from the material, I am sure that Darwin would have been happy to include it in the *Descent of Man*.

Strictly Darwinian or not, his influences can be seen in fiction, poetry, and cinema. For obvious reasons, real or quasi-dinosaur movies spring to mind, such as *Godzilla* or *Jurassic Park*. But there are also more thoughtful treatments of evolution. (*Godzilla* is pretty thoughtful, but it is more about the threat of atomic weapons than about evolution.) Think of the original *Planet of the Apes*, starring Charlton Heston as an astronaut who finds himself in a society run by apes—with the gorillas as the thugs, the chimpanzees as the intelligent but rather flighty members of society, and the orangutans as leaders of the clan. These are themes that would have done Thomas Hardy or Jack London proud. How can one not like a movie where Heston, the archetypal Hollywood he-man, fresh off gigs as Moses and Ben Hur, is threatened with gelding in the name of science?

Knowledge

Let's move on now to some of the areas where Darwin himself made specific claims. He was convinced that human brains, thoughts, and actions were molded by natural selection. In the past half a century or so, Darwinian biologists have explored these issues, and the whole new disciplines of cultural evolution have started to crystallize. With respect to knowledge itself, the most obvious route taken is that of the Pragmatists, who see ideas as things subject to selection and, hence, evolving. If the Darwinian process is one of putting up new variations and then subjecting them to the fire of the struggle for existence, then is not knowledge acquisition something very similar? Scientists come up with new ideas, put them into the general discourse, and then see how they fare. Not surprisingly, good ideas succeed, while bad ones are discarded. It is not a matter of ultimate truth or falsity, but much more a pragmatic matter of what works. Although I think Darwin yearned for an absolute truth, there are elements of this kind of thinking in the work of the great philosopher of science Sir Karl Popper—throw up your hypotheses and try to falsify them, and go for the "survivors." Similar kind of thinking is to be found in the systems based on Richard Dawkins's idea of "memes"—heritable units of culture that function much like genes, heritable units of biology. However, as many critics have pointed out, it is difficult to quantify this kind of thinking—a *sine qua non* of modern science—not to mention that it is less Darwinian and more Lamarckian, since the units of culture seem not to arrive randomly but only with thought and effort. (It is interesting and significant that Popper was an enthusiast for the ideas of the novelist Samuel Butler, an ardent Lamarckian.)

Samuel Butler (1835-1902), the author of Erewhon and The Way of All
Flesh. Initially, Butler was a great enthusiast for the ideas of Darwin, but
then things turned sour and rather personal, and Butler ended criticizing
both natural selection and its author. The second of his novels is a
searing semi-autobiographical account of a highly dysfunctional family
where Lamarckian themes keep surfacing, usually to the discomfort of
those affected.

A more direct biologically oriented approach, which goes now under the name of "evolutionary psychology," is one that Darwin proposed, even if he then did little with it. Our brains are not blank slates, *tabula rasa*—as argued by the English philosopher John Locke—but molded and shaped by the past. As Darwin wrote on August 16, 1838, "Origin of man now proved. Metaphysic must flourish. He who understands baboon would do more towards metaphysics than Locke." The following month, he noted: "Plato says in Phaedo that our *'necessary ideas'* arise from the preexistence of the soul, are not derivable from experience—read monkeys for preexistence." Actually, Darwin speculated in this way just before he hit on selection, but it is easy to see how it can be translated into selection-mode. One can argue that the ways in which we think and reason are a reflection of adaptive strategies that proved successful in our past. Even scientific reasoning has its justification in evolution. Why should we take something like a consilience of inductions to be a good form of reasoning? Simply because only those proto-humans who thought in consilient ways tended to survive and reproduce. The humans who took full account of all the clues and reasoned (let us say) that they point to an unseen-but-hovering predator stood a better chance of living than those who simply ignored the clues. They may have been happy in their ignorance, but their lives tended to be short.

David Hull (1935-2010) left and Michael Ruse (b. 1940) right, two ardent Darwinian philosophers who fortunately throve on criticism, which was just as well because that is what their thinking earned.

It is from such simple beginnings that everything else is built. Do not succumb to parody. No one is saying, for instance, that belief in the Darwinian account of origins is going to lead to more children than belief in the Genesis account–I suspect that evangelicals have more offspring than scientists–but rather than the foundations of the systems, and the methodology used to obtain them, are rooted in biology. Suggestive evidence from standard psychological experiments shows that when presented with situations demanding logic and reason, often we have no trouble with familiar cases, such as being in a bar, who is over and who is underage, and who can, therefore, order alcoholic drinks. On the other hand, we have trouble with formally identical but unfamiliar cases–what numbers are on the other sides of cards, and that sort of thing. One is still in a sense a Pragmatist. Darwinian evolution does not care about absolute truth; it does care about surviving and reproducing. Or as the old joke goes, if you are in a forest being chased by a bear, it does not matter how fast you run, just that you run faster than the person next to you.

Morality

The great philosopher Immanuel Kant said: "Two things fill the mind with ever new and increasing admiration and awe, the oftener and more steadily we reflect on them: the starry heavens above me and the moral law within me." In his novel, *The Call of the Wild*, the previously mentioned author Jack London told a tale of success and failure, and the impression we get is that London rather approves of his character Buck–a domesticated St. Bernard/Scotch Shepherd mix–in a way that he does not of Buck's archrival Spitz, the last stepping stone on Buck's way to becoming Master of the Universe, or, at least, Master of the Pack! As Thomas Henry Huxley would have told us, there was a moral element here. London was an enthusiast for what has come to be known as Social Darwinism–a movement perhaps more correctly called Social Spencerianism–where one has a rather extreme libertarian or laissez-faire form of society, with the government playing a minor role, while individuals and organizations are allowed to fight for supremacy. In this respect, London was echoing some of Spencer's most enthusiastic supporters–American industrialists John D. Rockefeller and Andrew Carnegie foremost among them.

However, things were a little more complex than one might suspect from popular accounts. Not all who brought evolution to bear on social issues were libertarians. For instance, Alfred Russel Wallace was always a socialist. (Actually, so also was Jack London, which I suppose all goes to support the adage that genius consists in the ability to hold contradictory ideas simultaneously.) He, therefore, emphasized the group effects of natural selection, arguing that state support is biologically justified. And then there was the Russian anarchist Prince Peter Kropotkin. He argued that animals naturally developed a sense of "mutual aid." This also applied to humans, who would be best off in small societies without heavy government scrutiny. He thought that given such a social situation, human happiness would peak in a way that was not possible otherwise.

Today's many Darwin critics, notably the evangelical Christians to be discussed in a moment, make much of supposed links between Darwinian theory and the National Socialist movement that ruled Germany with an iron grip from 1933 to 1945. They argue that there is a direct link between the *Origin*, with its talk about the struggle for existence, and Hitler's demands for geographic expansion at the expense of nations of Eastern Europe. To be fair, something must have incited Hitler in his fight for supremacy, and it would be naive to pretend that nothing in Social Darwinian theories (whether or not these were due to Darwin himself) had any effect in this respect. However, there were clearly many other factors leading to the emergence of Nazism. For a start, in the 19th century, there was the *völkish* movement in Germany, which was obsessed with glorifying the past and looking forward to triumphs in the future. And think of all those rousing Wagnerian operas, although how anyone sees and hears the *Ring* as a stalking horse for the Third Reich eludes me. Then there were religious issues as well, and it is certainly not implausible to think that anti-Semitism was a driving force behind Nazi thinking. It is also worth mentioning that, although one does sometimes find Hitler parroting Social Darwinian ideas, in many respects the Nazis were deeply opposed to Darwin's thinking. For instance, the essence of evolution is that all humans are related, including Aryans and Jews. Nazi theorists realized this and for this reason, they had a distant attitude towards evolution. In short, one should be very wary of simplified examples of links between Darwin and the horrible social movements of the 20th century.

Is Social Darwinism alive and well today? Certainly not by that name; however, there are those who promote ethical and social ideals in the name of evolution. One of the best known in America today is Edward O. Wilson, whom we met in the last chapter as one of the founders of sociobiology. Wilson, who was raised as an evangelical Christian, is ardent in his belief that our evolutionary origins are highly significant, both explaining our ethical inclinations and pointing to the moral tasks that humankind faces today. In particular, he argues strongly that humans have evolved in symbiotic relationship with the rest of nature—a world of plastic would literally be fatal to us all—and he, therefore, claims that we have a moral obligation to preserve biodiversity. Faithful to his beliefs, in recent years, Wilson has been much involved in campaigns to preserve and protect the Brazilian rainforests.

An interesting paradox is that today there is an already thriving movement that takes and makes use of Wilson's science but rejects his philosophy! Given the social nature of the human species, it lends itself readily to such explanatory models as kin selection—why do we have the kinds of inheritance laws that we do, trying to pass on our bounty to those who carry our genes. The English novelist Ian McEwan has explored some of these themes in his fiction, particularly in *Enduring Love*. A hot-air balloon rises out of control, and all let go except one character who rises and then falls and dies.

I didn't know, nor have I ever discovered, who let go first. I'm not prepared to accept that it was me. But everyone claims not to have been first. What is certain is that if we had not broken ranks, our collective weight would have brought the balloon down to earth a quarter of the way down the slope a few seconds later as the gust subsided. But as I've said, there was no team, there was no plan, no agreement to be broken. No failure. So can we accept that it was right, every man for himself? Were we all happy afterwards that this was a reasonable course? We never had that comfort, for there was a deeper covenant, ancient and automatic, written in our nature. Co-operation—the basis of our earliest hunting successes, the force behind our evolving capacity for language, the glue of our social cohesion. Our misery in the aftermath was proof that we knew we had failed ourselves. But letting go was in our nature too. Selfishness is also written on our hearts. This is our mammalian conflict—what to give to the others, and what to keep for yourself. Treading that line, keeping the others in check and being kept in check by them, is what we call morality. Hanging a few feet above the Chilterns escarpment, our crew enacted morality's ancient, irresolvable dilemma: us, or me.

I am not sure whether McEwan solves the dilemma in a satisfactory manner or not. The point here is that Darwinian themes inform his story. Similar turns to Darwinism can be found in the writings of many philosophers. The most celebrated moral system of the last half of the 20th century was John Rawls's theory of justice. As this American thinker noted, to be just we must be fair, and to be fair, we should put ourselves behind the "veil of ignorance." If we did not know our position in society, how would we want our society structured? If I knew I was going to be young and healthy and male, then I would want such people to get maximum benefits. But what if I am none of these? A just society speaks to such issues. Except, of course, no one thinks that there was really a veil of ignorance, so why should one take this sort of thing seriously? As Rawls wrote in 1971:

> In arguing for the greater stability of the principles of justice I have assumed that certain psychological laws are true, or approximately so. I shall not pursue the question of stability beyond this point. We may note however that one might ask how it is that human beings have acquired a nature described by these psychological principles. The theory of evolution would suggest that it is the outcome of natural selection.

Where we go from here—if, indeed, we can go anywhere—is a matter of considerable controversy. The important thing to note is that in philosophy, as in science, Darwin is, at last, being taken seriously. Do note also that today's would-be "evolutionary ethicists" have diverged from Huxley. They are arguing that morality emerges from the struggle rather than that morality demands combatting the struggle. Our sense of right and wrong is just as much a part of our heritage as our darker sides. Apostle St. Paul was right to see the life of the human as a conflict between emotions. In Romans 7:15, he is quoted saying, "I do not understand what I do. For what I want to do I do not do, but what I hate I do." What he missed mentioning was that nineteen hundred years later, an Englishman called Charles Darwin was going to show him why we behave this way.

American religion

We come to our final topic. Even though there was some initial objection to the message of the *Origin*, by about 1870 even religious people were familiar with Darwinism. Their reactions to it varied. Some accepted the ideas graciously, others less so; some accepted the concepts at first and then turned away; some found the whole experience painful and troubling, and others barely knew that anything significant had happened. However, even the Catholic Church had accepted the fact that Darwinian evolution was here to stay, although as we saw later for political reasons it had second thoughts. (Today, Catholics have no trouble with evolution.) There was one big exception. In the 19th century, Americans saw the emergence of a home-grown form of Protestant, evangelical Christianity, which was firmly Bible-based and insisted on reading the creation stories of Genesis in a very literal fashion. There were many reasons for the development of this movement, not the least of which were the quarrels both before and after the Civil War. In the South before the war, the Bible was taken as justification for slavery. Then, after the Confederate defeat, the Bible was used as justification for the troubled state of the South. Sermon after sermon was preached on the theme that God afflicts those he loves the most, and explicit analogies were drawn between the Israelites in captivity in Babylon and the South pressured by outsiders from the North.

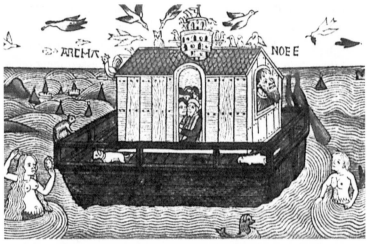

Noah's Ark, from a 1483 bible. *The reason Creationists focus on the Flood rather than other stories in Genesis is because it marks the end of a period, a dispensation, and it is thought that it mirrors Armageddon about to come—"as a thief in the night."*

Evolution was added to this mix. After the war, in the North, there was a great drive towards industrialism, education, and science generally. Evolution was taken to be the epitome of the underlying philosophy of progress and was embraced by the general population as well as by their leaders. In the post-war South, however, there was a longing for the past and determination to slough off changes imposed from outside. Evolution was as important to Southerners as it was to Northerners, but in the South, it was taken as a symbol of all that went wrong. Therefore, it had to be disproved in every possible way.

This conflict continued into and through the 20th century. In 1925 in the state of Tennessee, a young schoolteacher named John Thomas Scopes was prosecuted for teaching evolution to his students. The lead prosecutor in what had become known as "Scopes Trial" was the three-time presidential candidate William Jennings Bryan. Representing Scopes was the notorious agnostic lawyer Clarence Darrow. Both sides claimed victory. Scopes was found guilty, but the conviction was overturned on a technicality. The South took the trial as a symbol of defiance. The North saw it as a symbol of the importance of science and the crudity of thinking in the South. One chilling effect was that, after the Scopes trial, evolution was pretty much banished from textbooks and from any teaching in the nation's schools. Paradoxically, this happened as much in the North as in the South, because textbook manufacturers tended to produce one uniform edition, dumbed down to the lowest acceptable level.

Creationism

Biblical literalism, particularly focusing on the absolute truth of the Genesis stories of Creation, revived strongly after the Second World War. Americans were terrified of nuclear conflict with the Russians. Thus, an evangelical religion that focused on cataclysmic events in the past–most notably the Biblical flood and premonitions of Armageddon to come–found a ready market. Genesis Flood, published in 1961, authored by biblical scholar John C. Whitcomb and hydraulic engineer Henry M. Morris, was a runaway bestseller. Creationism, or as it was sometimes called, Scientific Creation, found many adherents, paradoxically just at the time when Darwinian evolution was finally moving forward rapidly as a fully-fledged, professional science.

There were bound to be clashes. In 1981, in the state of Arkansas, a law was passed insisting that schoolchildren be taught Creationism along with Evolution. Thanks to the US Constitution separating church and state, it was soon found illegal and overturned. By the 1990s, a new version of literalism was being promoted. So-called "Intelligent Design Theory" claims that there are aspects of the organic world that are "irreducibly complex" and thus, cannot be explained by natural means. The motor driving the tail, the "flagellum," on bacteria was one example. One must, therefore, invoke a designer, and, although the proponents tended to be rather cagey on the subject, there was little doubt that this designer was to be identified with the God of the Bible. Again a court case occurred and again literalism was pushed back. But it continues to thrive today.

Interestingly, in recent years, evolutionists have gone in parallel directions to the Creationists, inasmuch as they have entered the public domain and started to argue strongly for the imposition of their views against all alternatives. Undoubtedly sparked by the horrors of 9/11, when Muslim terrorists flew planes into the World Trade Center and the Pentagon, these fanatics have argued vehemently not just for evolution but also against all forms of Christianity and other religions. The leader of the so-called "New Atheists" is Richard Dawkins, the author of *The Selfish Gene* and *The God Delusion*.

Just as in the late 19th-century evolution was taken as a banner for modernity, for the new Atheists today evolution has a very similar role. And we find a counter in the Intelligent Design Theorists, who usually cannot wait to move on from the fossil record to condemnations of modern life, including abortion on demand and gay marriage. The paradox is that, although Charles Darwin would almost certainly have agreed with many of the claims made by the New Atheists, he would've drawn back with horror from their tactics. Ever the English gentleman, Darwin would have thought that it was socially crude and politically inopportune to attack Christianity in the open way advocated by Dawkins and his supporters. Although, to be fair, he was not living in a world where his opponents argued that his thinking led straight to the Third Reich and the concentration camps.

This clash over evolution is continuing, and no resolution is yet in sight. Until recently, it was very much an American phenomenon. However, increasingly it is being exported to other countries as well. For instance, Creationism of various kinds has found receptive ears in several Muslim nations, and there too evolution is a symbol of all that is wrong. Likewise in Britain and in Australia, one finds enthusiasts for Creationism and attempts to introduce it into the schools. It is surely paradoxical that, at a time when evolutionary biology has matured into one of the most important areas of natural science, in the public domain it should be under ever-increasing pressures.

Conclusion

Debates are ongoing and probably will be for quite some time. There are those who are enthusiastic Darwinians. There are those who are not. But for or against, no one denies that Darwin's ideas stimulate and provoke. For that reason if for no other, no educated person today should be ignorant of the life and labors of Charles Darwin. In science and in culture, he is one of the seminal figures of all time. I hope I have shown you also that his ideas are not just important—they are incredibly interesting as well.

Charles Darwin in old age by the famed Victorian photographer Julia Margaret Cameron.

Suggested Reading

E ven before the *Origin of Species* was published in 1859, Charles Darwin was already a well-known figure in Britain and beyond. He became famous thanks to his wonderfully engaging 1839 book, *Voyage of the Beagle*, which documented the British naturalist's trip around the world. The *Voyage* is a terrific read, well worth your time.

The *Origin*, expectedly, demands more effort, but for a major contribution to the history of science, it is remarkably easy to read and follow. There are many editions, but (because Darwin wrote and rewrote the work, over the years, not always wisely) scholars today strongly recommend a reprint of the first edition—Harvard University Press puts out a facsimile edition with an introduction by the noted 20th-century evolutionist, Ernst Mayr.

Even during his lifetime, people were writing about Darwin and his ideas, and in the years since his death in 1882, there has been a huge output, both by supporters and opponents of his theory. The last half a century has seen some very sophisticated studies, helped by the fact that Darwin hoarded every scrap of paper, so there are notebooks, unpublished (at the time) essays, and literally thousands of letters, both to Darwin and from him.

For anyone who wants to learn seriously about Darwin, the essential starting place is the two-volume biography by Janet Browne: *Charles Darwin: Voyaging* (1995) and *Charles Darwin: The Power of Place* (2002). The first volume takes us up to the *Origin*; since it covers the *Beagle* voyage, as well as the discovery of natural selection, it is very exciting. The second volume is invaluable too as a guide—not just to Darwin's own life and work after the *Origin*, but also for insights into the ways in which his ideas spread and were (or were not) accepted both by professional scientists and the general public.

A best-selling account of Darwin's life is *Darwin: The Tormented*

Evolutionist (1992), by Adrian Desmond and James R. Moore. Even the authors—especially the authors—know that this work goes over the top much of the time. For a start, although Darwin was sick for most of his adult life, he was far from tormented, as this particular book infers. He had a happy family life, the respect of the professional community, and the realization that he had made one of the all-time great discoveries of Western thought. He was rich, so he had no financial pressures like his friend and supporter Thomas Henry Huxley, for instance. And although Darwin thought much about religion, he never worried about it unduly—he admitted that he slid comfortably from faith to non-belief.

Yet, for a feel of the period and a torrent of previously uncovered fascinating material, *Darwin: The Tormented Evolutionist* is not to be missed. Reading the book is a bit like eating hot, salted, boiled peanuts. Their nutritional value might be questionable, but no one can stop eating them until they are finished.

In the past several decades, historian of biology Peter Bowler has made a career out of trashing the Darwinian Revolution, arguing that it was not a real revolution and that even if it was, it can't be attributed to Darwin. An early onslaught included *The Non-Darwinian Revolution: Reinterpreting a Historical Myth* (1988); the most recent is *Darwin Deleted: Imagining a World Without Darwin* (2013). I am a great believer in letting a thousand flowers bloom, or, in Popperian language, making bold conjectures. I have even blurbed Bowler's books, inviting people to read them. I am also a supporter of cutting down 999 of those flowers—or in Popperian language—offering rigorous refutations. We learn from our mistakes, and Bowler provides a great learning experience.

Obviously, this little book is aimed against the Bowler thesis. I take up the matter in more detail in *Darwinism as Religion: What Literature Tells Us About Religion* (2016) and also in *Debating Darwin: Mechanist or Romantic?* (2016). The latter is co-authored with Robert J. Richards—we write separate essays and responses—and my contribution also takes on Richards' equally mistaken notion that there was a Darwinian Revolution, but that it owed more to ethereal Germanic Romantic philosophy than to the bread-and-butter beliefs of English empiricists and social scientists.

As you will learn quickly, having lots of materials to draw on encourages controversy and disagreement rather than promoting harmony and uniformity. Thank goodness!

Looking for an overview, let me recommend to you a massive volume I edited recently, *The Cambridge Encyclopedia of Darwin and Evolutionary Thought*. With over 60 contributors—including Bowler and Richards—it covers just about everything relating to Darwin: the background, the man and his work, the scientific reactions, the religious reactions, and much more, including extensive discussions of how Darwin's thinking holds up today. There is also a very extensive bibliography. For online resources, let me recommend the web page *Darwin Online*, http://darwin-online.org.uk/, run by the indefatigable John van Wyhe. It has a huge amount of published and unpublished material, as well as many very useful essays. And if you are still looking for more material, then the online "Oxford Bibliographies," http://www.oxfordbibliographies.com are invaluable. There are entries on Darwin himself, on Darwinism, on Evolution and its history, on Creationism, on just about every branch of Evolution today, and much, much more. I wrote most of them—at least, it felt that way at the time—so I recommend them heartily! More seriously, the world of Darwin scholarship is incredibly supportive and so by the time the entries were finished, nearly everyone had had his say, so the information really is comprehensive and well balanced.

About the Author

Michael Ruse is the Lucyle T. Werkmeister Professor of Philosophy and Director of the Program in the History and Philosophy of Science at Florida State University. He is the author or editor of more than fifty books, including *The Gaia Hypothesis: Science on a Pagan Planet*, *The Cambridge Encyclopedia of Darwin and Evolutionary Thought* and *Atheism: What Everyone Needs to Know*.

A Word from the Publisher

Thank you for reading *Simply Darwin*!

If you enjoyed reading it, we would be grateful if you could help others discover and enjoy it too.

Please review it with your favorite book provider such as Amazon, BN, Kobo, iBooks and Goodreads, among others.

Again, thank you for your support and we look forward to offering you more great reads.

CPSIA information can be obtained
at www.ICGtesting.com
Printed in the USA
BVHW030011090620
581041BV00001B/7